Minimalist
Budget

*Simple and Practical
Budgeting Strategies to
Save Money, Avoid
Compulsive Spending,
Pay Off Debt and Simplify
Your Life*

Marie S. Davenport

Table of Contents

Introduction

If you have ever struggled with your
monthly budget—to pay your bills, to
make ends meet, to get out of debt, or
even to dream a life where you can
thrive financially—you are not alone. In
fact, 80.9% of baby boomers, 79.9% of
Gen Xers, and 81.5% of millennials are
living with debt. That's 8 out of every 10
people you meet struggling to get the
money monster off their back. The good
news is that there is hope, and the
answer doesn't even begin with your
bank account—it begins with your
mindset. Modern society trains us to be
consumers without limit, and it is no
wonder why so many feel helpless when
it comes to the health of their finances.
No matter what stage of life you are in, it

is not too late to overhaul your budget, to make real financial gains, and to start shaping your life with prosperity mindset.

The *Minimalist Budget* addresses the underlying fears and habits that are preventing you from feeling relieved about your finances. The process begins not by attacking your credit cards, student loans, mortgages, or medical bills blindly, but by first discovering that you have more resources than you realize. By changing your mindset from fear to abundance, you can start feeling more powerful and more confident about making the changes that will improve your finances. The simple and straightforward advice here in *Minimalist Budget* will empower you to stop letting your days be dictated by impulse spending, denial budgeting, and despair about your future.

Chapter 1: Getting Started with a Minimalist Budget

Chapter 1: Getting Started with a Minimalist Budget

1.1

What is everybody's first reaction when a bank card application is declined? Embarrassment. We don't want those around us to think that we don't have money. Suze Orman, a financial expert, says that anger, fear, and shame are the most common emotions that surround money.

Everybody believes that money is just about your bank balance. It is, but it is also connected very strongly to emotions. And before you start believing that you are exempted from these emotions, think again.

What is your emotion when you realize that you are at your last penny? Depression, panic, fear, and anger.

There are times when our emotions towards money become so strong that we begin to hate money because we think it is causing all of our problems. Hate is a pretty strong emotion. Money has also been a reason for some people who have tried to commit suicide.

How would you feel if you inherited a large sum of money or won the lottery? You'll feel elated, probably—relieved, no more money problems—even free, or so you think.

A sudden large sum of money changes people. Money gives them a status and makes them feel powerful. Suddenly, they start to have an air of arrogance. Money can also influence the way someone treats those around them. If a homeless person were to walk into a high-end store, chances are somebody is going to shoo them out. If a person that has a nice suit on and drives a BMW walks into the same store, they'll get the red carpet rolled out for them. People respect those that are wealthy. As sad as this may seem, it is true. That's the power of money.

Our views of money often come from our childhood. The way our parents handled money gave us our foundation for the way we handle money now. This is why generational wealth and poverty exist. Poor people impart their money habits to their children. The same goes for wealthy people. Along with this problem is the fact that poor people are unable to further their children's education.

But the truth is: money isn't the problem. The problem comes from the way you approach money, how you handle money, and how you think about money. People who are constantly negative when it comes to money are always going to be plagued by money issues. Those who think that they can control money are the ones that end up becoming successful and further increase their money. Those are the type of people that, instead of complaining about the money they don't have, educate themselves. Financial intelligence is how you grow wealth.

Changing your financial situation will

start with changing how you think about money. It is important that you clear out your negative thoughts about money and get rid of blockages.

While you need to examine your feelings about money and become better at managing it, you need to make sure that you don't let it consume you. Money must not become the center of your life because this can be detrimental to your quality of life, family, and health.

This is why a minimalist budget can help. Before I tell you what it is, let's go over what it's not.

It won't teach you how to maximize credit card deals, coupons, rewards, or any other consumer freebie that will require you to open multiple accounts. It won't help you save the most money or make you a frugal person. It will, however, help you simplify your finances so that you will have an easier system to achieve your financial goals.

1.2

You may be asking why a minimalist budget works. It helps you keep your finances simple so that you are able to pay off your bills, add to your savings, and give you the freedom to use the money for fun things. It is also a great place for budgeting novices to start. You don't have to worry about uncertainty— you will have clear action steps, and it will also be able to provide you with your investment, savings, and financial goals. This is the reason why you will be more likely to stick to the plan until you reach your desired goal of financial stability.

A minimalist budget will also give you some flexibility. You are able to bend things a bit so that it works better for you. You don't have to be exact about how things work because budgets will differ from one person to another. The important thing is to take action and make use of a system that helps you remain consistent in managing your monthly income and to make sure that you cover the expenses that you need to. You are responsible for your savings, and you have some wiggle room to enjoy life.

1.3

Now that you have an idea of what a minimalist budget is, let's look at some ways that you can do to start changing your life and improving your finances.

1. **Change the way you view borrowing or payments to owning.**

   There are a lot of people who are "broke" that will talk about owning things in terms of payments. They say things like "I got the car because there was a great deal on the lease. My monthly payments are only $200." Their goals are to stretch out their finances as much as they can so that they can live beyond their means with a lifestyle that they feel entitled to but are not able to afford.

With a minimalist budget, you will be required to flip this kind of view upside-down. Instead of looking at things in terms of payments, you have to view things in terms of ownership. Don't ask about monthly payments; instead, ask what it would cost to buy it outright.

This can be done by believing that your income potential is limitless, not being frugal, and staying away from credit cards. This is very different from the majority of people, but it is the best way to gain financial freedom.

2. **Establish financial priorities, and define financial values.**

To be able to get rid of unnecessary things, you have to figure out what is unnecessary to you. This means that you will have to define everything that is important to you. After you have figured out what you really value the most, you can then come up with financial priorities. Some examples of financial values are:

a. Retire by the age of 55.
b. Donate 10% of your income to your favorite charity.
c. Have a 30% buffer between expenses and income.
d. Save 20% of your monthly income.

e. Live debt-free.

After you have decided on what your values are, you will then establish your priorities. These priorities are basically your financial goals. These are your plan for moving from where you are to where you are going to be. These are going to vary based on your current status.

Some examples would be:

1. Come up with a long-term plan that will give you the opportunity to retire at 55.
2. Make 20% more money by doing something on the side.
3. Start to donate 10% to

your favorite charity.

4. Once you have repaid all of
   your debt, start saving
   20% of your income.

5. Pay off your debt in three
   years.

These are only a few examples.
There are a lot of things you can
do to create your own priorities.
When you aren't sure of what you
want, following a 50/20/30
budget is a great idea, and we will
go into that in chapter seven.

Another thing you need to look at
is the value of experience as
compared to physical things.
Research has found that people
are happier when they spend
money on experiences instead of

spending their money on material things. It's easy for it to feel like buying things is the only way to be happy, especially in American culture. However, this isn't true, so fight that feeling. Start prioritizing experiences over things.

It's extremely important that you figure out your values and define your priorities so that you can come up with a minimalist budget. The foundation of this way of living is prioritizing the things that are important and forgetting all the other things.

3. **Live simply with fewer credit cards and accounts.**

A person with a minimalist budget will normally have one main checking and one main savings account. The checking account is needed for discretionary and non-discretionary expenses. The savings account will be used as an emergency fund.

If you need to have a credit card, only have one. You may give up some rewards, but you will be making your life simpler and making things easier for you to stay organized and on top of your spending.

This is the biggest area where people make mistakes. There are people that own seven-plus savings and checking accounts; one for an emergency, one for down payment, one for taxes, and so on. It gets messy, and normally they will end up borrowing from one to fund another. Then, there are some people who are stuck in payment mode. They have payments going in a million different directions, and they are barely saving anything.

4. Think twice before you purchase.

When you have a minimalist budget, you have to question all of your purchases. Ask yourself if it is absolutely necessary. Keep in mind that it will take some time for you to earn money, so all of

your purchases need to be worth
the time you spent making that
money.

5. Schedule financial meetings.

It's one thing to organize your
finances and to have a plan; it's
another thing to implement it.
There are some things in your life
that are going to change and will
make your plan unworkable.

It's important that you review,
revise, and evaluate your budget
regularly to keep things working.
Set a monthly financial meeting
with yourself and with your
spouse if you have one. This gives
you time to change your budget.

6. **Be okay with feeling like a weirdo.**

Others may think that you are being completely weird, so get used to it. What you're doing is a good thing. You are living intentionally, and you have a plan for your money. A lot of people don't do this, and if they judge you, it's just because they don't understand it.

7. **Keep Up with Your Spending for the Previous Month**

Figuring out just where all of your money has gone during the past month is going to be one of the longest and time-consuming things you will have to do.

Luckily, this will only have to be done once a month, so suck it up and get on with it. Gather up all of your bank statements, receipts, and credit card statements from the previous month. Now, you need to come up with budget categories and then match up your spending.

If this doesn't seem like something that you want to do by hand, there are plenty of online money management tools that can help you do this. Some of the budget categories that you must create include:

- Savings
- Debt payments – student loans, car loans, credit cards,

and so on.

- Insurance
- Living expenses – utilities, rent, and the like
- Entertainment
- Food
- Miscellaneous

In later chapters, we will go further in depth on all of these different categories that you will have to figure out.

8. Give your Money a New Direction

Hopefully, you have a pretty good goal that will help you stay motivated with your new minimalist budget. This will help you go full-force into redirecting your money. Once you have taken a good look at your spending patterns, you must have a pretty good idea as to where all of your money is going—so now, how much do you have left to spend once you reach the end of the month?

If there isn't any extra money to spend, then you will have to cut back on some of your spendings. When you make these cuts, you need to make sure that you are realistic. If you know that you are going to spend $50 on gas each week, then don't choose that area to cut back. This is only going to be setting yourself up for failure.

Instead, choose areas to cut back

on that will be less painful. This can mean groceries. You may be spending too much money on entertainment things. You must never cut back on your debt repayments, but all of the other categories can and must be cut back on if at all possible.

Your Quick Start Action Step:

To help you get started on this right now, here are few quick action steps that you can start doing right this minute.

1. **Come up with a list of your spending, and evaluate your consumption.**

Come up with a list of everything that you spend your money on. The more detailed you can make this, the better it will be. After you have created your list, evaluate every item. Ask if that item adds something meaningful to your life. Do you value the item? Does it help you achieve your priorities and values?

Keep in mind that when you say yes to something, you will be saying no to something else. When you say yes to something that adds no value, you are saying no to yourself.

Let's assume that you spend $150 every month on your hair. Ask yourself if spending this is serving your end priorities and values. If it isn't helping you in that manner, is it something that you find more important than your future? You can say yes, or you can say no. The important thing to understand is that when you spend this money on certain stuff, you have to eliminate spending elsewhere.

When you find that you are spending money on things that aren't in line with your financial future, you need to cut out those expenses.

2. **Come up with a spending plan.**

This involves listing out your

expenses and comparing them to your income. This is where you need to break down your expenses and income and figure out where you want to spend your money. Everybody has different expenses, so this is a personal thing that you have to come up with.

3. **Automate payments.**

Since minimalism involves making your finances more organized and simplified, it only makes sense that you automate your payments. You can also automate your savings, debt payments, and bills. The easier you can make your life under your new budget, the better.

Chapter 2: Shifting Your Mindset from Unnecessary Spending and Debt Build-Up to Simple and Smart Spending & Budgeting

2.1

Minimalism isn't discussed much in terms of its philosophies. It tends to be more talked about methodologically. In order to have a minimalist budget, it's important to get into a minimalist mindset. This is a mindset of someone who makes it a choice to live a minimal life and make it the root of their behavior.

This isn't just some mindless fad. How can it be when it requires a bit of sacrifice and some limitations? Generally, most people who make the decision to simplify their life do this because they start to think differently about how they can live their best life, or they notice the destructive and immoral nature of thoughtless consumerism and make that conscious effort to get rid of their own demons.

If you don't cultivate the right mindset, your budget is going to be a constant battle. You will try to resist those temptations. You will try to reduce mental and physical clutter. You will try to find solutions. But during all of this, your inner urges will grow. A lot like an extreme diet, minimalism without the right mindset will leave you destined to relapse. When you have to push against your own desires, it becomes a losing battle.

So if you're not supposed to fight against your own desires, what are you supposed to do? This isn't meant to tell you to give up on trying to live a simpler life. I want to make sure that you are realistic about this so that you can make your life easier. The right mindset for a minimalist budget isn't about fighting your desires; it's about learning how to not desire.

Once you have cultivated the right mindset, you will find that you are no longer fighting a losing battle. You will be driven by your motives, and your actions will fall into place. You will love the simplicity, and you will understand the reasons behind these actions.

This mindset is best seen as a reduction based on priorities. It doesn't mean that you have to get rid of and stop buying things that you enjoy and wish that you could have all of them back. It means that you will make reductions at a decent pace, and over time you will start to represent the things that are really important.

Objects and things are the most commonly pictured cut back, but when it comes to a minimalist mindset, it also applies to activities and relationships—including with yourself, speech, and all aspects of your life. You will learn to make reductions based on priorities. This will make room for the things that really matter to you.

2.2

Most people don't understand why you want to live a life within a minimalist budget. They don't understand why you aren't taking advantage of all the luxuries and invention that are available.

They believe they have earned the right to live however they want and by any means necessary. This is true. What they don't understand is that living a life with a minimalist budget will benefit you in ways that they don't understand.

1. **Decluttering will help you breathe.**

    When you start reducing the things you buy and start getting rid of things in your home, it will open up more space in your life. You find that you have more room to move around. More importantly, you will no longer be holding onto things that aren't giving you anything. You'll find new freedom in less stuff cluttering your life, and this includes those credit card bills. All of this means you will be able to breathe easier.

2. **Minimalism will give you the chance to refocus.**

When you have a lot of stuff, your focus will be everywhere. You are constantly worried about making enough money to pay for everything, and you spend your time looking for places to put away everything. When all of this stuff is gone and your bills are lessened, it will become possible for you to focus your energy and time on things that are important, like the things and people around you.

3. **Buying less means more money.**

When you start cutting back on things, other things will open up. The money that you will have spent buying things you don't need, maintaining things, and making sure you have the latest stuff, will be in your pocket and not in a store. You will be able to pay off your debts, and you will eventually free up even more money. You will depend on money a lot less.

4. **You will have more time.**

When you require less money to live, you won't have to work as much. This will give you more time. You also won't have to spend as much time dealing with those extra things. You will be able to focus on your time so that you can do the things you enjoy.

5. You will have more energy.

When you don't have all the clutter, the energy you will have spent dealing with all of this will become available for other things. People who don't have to deal with a materialistic life are stronger and healthier as a result.

2.3

It can seem daunting to develop the right mindset for a minimalist budget, but with the right steps, you will be there in no time.

1. **Start Small**

If you are like the majority of Americans drowning in the debt of the American Dream, take a look at your bills and stuff, and wonder if you can even find freedom in all of this. The first thing you need to do is to focus on one small area that you can purge. This can be as simple as your purse or wallet. This is just one step that is manageable and will set you up for success in the long run.

Instead of thinking that you must do everything in one fell swoop, do things in little chunks. Budget your time each day to accomplish something that will get you closer to your minimalist budget. Your hard work is going to build up, and you will be amazed at how little effort it will take.

2. Assign Value

If you want to have a successful minimalist budget, you have to learn how to figure out the value of things. Creating this budget will involve fixing up your house as well as your bank account. When you go through your house and clean out things, you may find yourself faced with the question, "what if I need it later?"

Having a minimalist mindset means you will have to figure out what are the things that are essential, and you can't do that without understanding your ultimate purpose. If you aren't going to find meaning and success in the things that you have, where will you look? How are you going to design your life to find them? It will probably take some mind retraining to place value on things that you can't actually touch. Maybe instead of purchasing stuff, you decide you want to pursue outdoor adventures, physical fitness, or generosity. Whatever it is that gives your life purpose, keep it your focus and center yourself on that.

3. Watch Out for Sentimentality

Gifts from birthdays and holidays, especially kid's gifts, can easily pile up for anybody. No matter what causes the pileup, a lot of people will have trouble managing these things. A lot of people will feel guilty about getting rid of these things, especially those gifts that you are meant to figure out what to do with. Family heirlooms have the same kind of weight. It depends on whether they hold any real value.

Try taking photos of things that you are sentimental about. This will give you something to remember it by without it taking up your time and money to maintain.

4. Stop Comparing

This is the hard-learned truth when it comes to living within your means. Yes, you need to quit making a comparison. Most people think that they have to have something to measure up to somebody else. Instead of looking at what other people are doing, try looking at yourself. Get rid of Facebook for 30 days, avoid going to the malls, and stop reading luxurious magazines. Find out what you need. You will probably find that it isn't much stuff.

5. Check Your Cart

With online shopping, it is extremely easy to accumulate a lot of stuff you don't need and waste money. Instead of checking out as soon as you have found the things you *need*, leave those items in your cart for a few days or weeks even. In the majority of the time, you will discover that you have forgotten about them never really needed them, to begin with. This works anytime that there is a chance for an impulse buy.

6. Remove the Value of Your Purchases

Everything that we buy will hold some sort of value for our lives. That means it's up to use to figure out what is actually necessary versus what is superfluous when we are buying things. For example, you may be buying food because you actually need to eat or because you are just bored and want to eat. You may go clothes shopping and buy things that you want because they are trendy, or you may buy clothes that you actually need. You may buy a glass of wine because you actually want one, or you may get one just because everybody else around you is having a glass, and you don't want to feel left out.

The important thing is to

remember these wise words, "you can't have everything you want, but you can love everything you have." View life as if you were traveling full-time on a budget. It will change the way you buy services and goods. You will have to justify the costs to support your lifestyle. You will be less likely to buy all of those souvenirs and little knick-knacks that you like but won't be useful for you. Everything you buy will likely have many different uses. For example, clothing items will probably match with the majority of your wardrobe, charging cables must work on multiple devices, and how much you spend on certain items will depend on how useful and how long you plan on using them.

When you purchase things with a critical eye, it will help you evaluate how much value, or lack thereof, a purchase will contribute to the quality of your life. Thinking twice about the things that you spend your money on and discovering ways to extract value from the things you buy will make sure that your purchases will end up being deliberate, being put to good use, and being worth the money you spend on them.

Your Quick Start Action Step:

If you're trying to really supercharge that minimalist mindset right now, here are a few tips.

1. **Get Inspired**

    Go online and look at minimalist
    spaces, or you can read some
    blogs or magazines that focus on
    this type of thing.

2. **Have More Experience**

    Millennials sort of already have
    this down. They are interested in
    having experiences instead of
    having stuff. Try spending any
    extra income you have on doing
    things instead of getting things,s
    and see if this makes you feel
    better.

3. **Find Encouragement in**

Community

Chances are that the struggles you have faced and will face as you transition to a minimalist budget lifestyle isn't anything new. Somebody else has probably gone through this before. Reach out to those people for help and inspiration.

4. Practice!

This is a journey that will never stop. You have to work on it little by little. Start saying no to more and more things, and it will become easier. The same goes for getting rid of things. Become aware of how this will make you even happier. Don't get upset if

you notice that these things feel
like a challenge.

Chapter 3: Reviewing Your Personal Finances

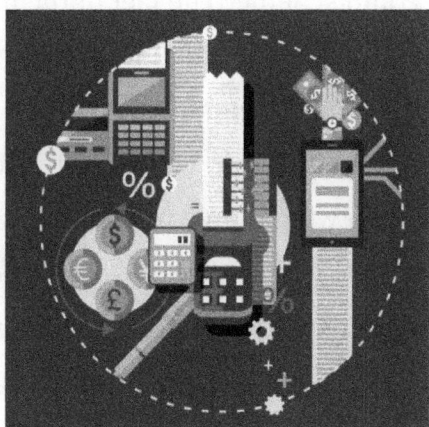

3.1

Having a budget may sound like an unrealistic and simplistic way to manage your income. There are some people who may think that it is ineffective in the grand scheme. The fact of the matter is, budgets don't work unless you make them work. You can handle this by sitting down, coming up with it, and then reviewing it on a regular basis.

You won't know the effectiveness of it until you have given it a try. If you are currently struggling to make ends meet, balance what you make with what you spend then save money. This will be a lot easier if you allocate your budget.

This doesn't mean that you just make it, but you also have to actively use it.

Your budget can range from simple to complex. There are loads of software available that can help you come up with your budget that works with your personal needs and lifestyle. You can even use a blank word document or a piece of paper.

After you have come up with your budget, the next important thing that you have to do is to review it on a regular basis. If it's not reviewed regularly, you won't know if it is still working for you. Budgets are ongoing, changing, and working documents that will change along with your life.

3.2

You have to remember that keeping a budget and reviewing it regularly isn't about deprivation. It's about making sure you stay proactive in the way that you use your money. You need to find creative ways to get the most out of it while you stick to the plan that is designed to give you a chance to live well and save adequately while living with peace of mind and surplus.

If you are brand new to your budgeting process, you will find that the first few months are going to be about coming up with your goals and setting them as realistically as you can. If you intend on meeting all of your goals, you will likely have to make a few adjustments. The longer you maintain your budget, the less frequent these adjustments will become.

Another important thing about your

monthly review is that if you are married, make sure you do these reviews together. It's fine if one of you wants to take the lead in getting the numbers together, but you both share in the decision-making process and, likely, the money-making process. Oftentimes, financial disagreements are caused by assumptions about who spent what. Looking at the numbers every month will do wonders for clarity and will foster teamwork and communication.

3·3

Understanding your budget and where your money is going is crucial for a minimalist budget. Make sure that you follow these steps to stay in control of your finances. Everything you do in this section and in the action steps will be helpful when you reach chapter seven and create your actual budget.

1. Review Your Spending

You need to make sure that you understand how you spend your money. This is the most important part of a review. This is going to help you work out where you are able to save some money.

Take a look at your bank statements. This can help you find most things that you have to spend money on using your credit or debit card. You will also be able to find the amount of cash that you take out every week.

In the future, it will be a good

idea to make a record of your spending. This is going to give you a better idea of where all of your money is being spent and how you can save some.

2. Identify Areas for Possible Savings

You may be able to reduce your bills for things such as your cell phone and electricity and not have to sacrifice on quality. You must also look at some of the most common ways that people tend to throw away money. And if you are going to college, you can check to see if you are paying for things that you can also be getting for free.

3. Find Help if You Need It

At this point, you must have a pretty good understanding of what your financial situation looks like, but if things are pretty serious, you may need to find some help.

If you are currently a student, with a little bit of research, you can find an emergency grant or loan. If you are majorly in debt, you can get some free advice from debt counselors on what you must do.

You may even find yourself considering a payday loan to help you make ends meet. These tend to be extremely expensive and

will likely just make your bad
situation even worse, so make
sure that you look carefully at
your alternatives.

4. Have You Looked at All of Your Expenses?

This may sound like a dumb
question, but more often than
not, this is the main thing that
will get people in trouble when it
comes to accounts and budgeting.

Sure, everybody is aware of their
typical expenses, such as gas,
electric, water, mortgage, and so
on. But it's also important that
you look at those once a month or
year expenses that don't
necessarily have a due date but

must be put into your budget, lest they are forgotten.

Some of these types of things may include medication, dog food, toiletries, yearly subscriptions to things like Amazon Prime and car registration. These types of things can end up running out at very random times, but it is absolutely necessary to purchase if you were to run out of toilet paper.

Since most of these aren't recurring expenses with a set due date, they are often easily needed when you aren't expecting them. And if all of your money has been set aside for the week on other needed items, these needs can easily catch you by surprise, and you will end up being unprepared. If you end up being unprepared, then your credit card will end up taking a hit.

The best thing for you to do is to sit down with your family and hash out all of the small expenses that may end up coming up during the year. Create a chart that has every month on it, and then write out all of these little expenses that may come up during the month. You can't leave anything out. These expenses may be school supplies (especially in the month of August) new clothes, or money to set aside for Halloween candy.

Then, for every succeeding month

of doing your budget, have this list ready so that you are able to account for each of these small expenses that will come up during the next month. It may even help if you break these expenses down by week. If you want to do this, all you need to do is add the expense to a specific line instead of just the month.

For example, let's assume that you are going to need $100 to get some new clothes for your children before school starts back. Decide on the week that you are going to go shopping and then place that purchase on that week's total. This will help you to make sure that you are prepared and that you will have plenty of money to get your job done, without ending up over budget.

If, after your first meeting, you or a family member discovers that there is another expense coming up in the next few months that you haven't accounted for, then add it into your list so that you are prepared.

You have to remember that there isn't an expense that is too small to worry about. If you make sure to think about it now, then there is a good chance that you won't be caught off guard when you are faced with the expense.

5. Are All of the Numbers Firm, or Can You Change Them?

This is a pretty hard question to answer, but it is a pretty relevant one. You have to know if any of the expenses that you have during the month are able to be changed—and if they are, will you be able to still make the payment?

For example, let's say that you just moved into a new house and are running your AC quite a bit. You average around $110 each month for your electric utilities, which works perfectly into your budget, so all is well.

However, the weather quickly gets colder. When this change happens, it causes a change in your electric bill, sending it all the way up to $150. This is a little bit higher than you have been used to, but you can still handle it with just a few little tweaks to your budget.

Then, say the next month, your bill jumps up to $229. The following month, you get a bill of $272. That puts you at over $160 than what you have been originally paying. To say the least, you will be quite shocked. Now, this is a new house, as we've stated earlier, so you will be better prepared the next year. But that still means you are going to have to do some strategic planning to get those bills paid now.

So how can you prevent this surprise? Go through all of your bills, and find those that can all of a sudden change on you. Most of your bills will probably have a flat rate, like $21 for trash pickup or $20 for internet, but there are some that are based on your usage of their service. The usual ones are cell phone service, water utilities, and electric utilities.

After you have figured out when bills can end up fluctuating, keep tabs on when they are more likely to change. With our example above, it will be a safe bet that the electric bill is going to go up quite a bit during the winter, so that means you will need to be more progressive with your budget from November to February so that you don't end up getting caught off guard when you get the bill.

Alongside this, you will also want to know where you are able to pull extra funds from just in case you do end up getting caught off guard. It's important that you always have a fallback if there is a time that a bill may trip you up. When you have a plan, you will be able to prevent late payments and charges, and you will be less likely to have to turn to your credit card to compensate for the difference.

6. Do You Have Enough

Spending Money for Unexpected Expenses?

This can be a big problem for people, especially if they have large amounts of credit card debt. There are a lot of people that will try to pay off their cards each month without incurring any interest, which means that they are going to have to sacrifice their spending money to hit what they need to each month. But when they do this, they are forcing themselves to have to use the credit card to make their monthly payments, which means that they are going to be stuck in a never-ending cycle.

It is extremely important that you

leave yourself plenty of spending money. If you are having to pay off debt, it can be extremely attractive to throw every penny you have to it. However, take this piece of advice: you will be paying off those credit cards for a lot longer if you don't allow yourself extra money first and then pay on the debt.

Make sure that every week, you give yourself some spending money. This can be left in your bank, and you can spend it from there. However, it is often better if you pull out the cash. Cash is very visual—so with just a glance, you will know exactly how much you have to spend, and you won't be able to overspend your cash like you can with a card.

The amount that you choose to keep on you for spending will depend on your family and your budget. Find what works best for you, and don't sacrifice. It's better to be prepared than to have to turn to credit when something unexpected comes up.

Your Quick Start Action Step:

The following are some quick action steps that you can make to get your finances under control.

1. **Check Your Bank Balance**

   This is the quickest and easiest thing you can do to take control of your money, and this can be one of the scariest things to know. You have to understand where your situation is, which means that you need to know the amount of money you have or the amount that you owe.

- Sign into your online bank account, and find out how much money you have left or how overdrawn you are.

- You will then need to look at other debts you may owe. This may mean credit cards or loans that you haven't paid off yet. You must not consider student loans because they work differently.

- Lastly, look at your savings to see what you have. It is best to leave these funds alone—but if you are in a lot of debt, you may want to use some of this to pay off them off because it can help you save more money in the long run. This is why it's important to know what you have.

2. **Check Your Income**

Understanding the amount of money that you earn in each month is important to understand your finances. The income you get each month can come from the money from your family, benefits, pay from work, scholarships, bursaries, and student loans.

You will probably receive money from different places at different times during the month. For example, your job may pay you every week or once a month, but your student loan will come in at the beginning of the term. To fully understand the amount you have to spend, try to work out the monthly or weekly equivalent for each of your income types. This is going to help you avoid spending your entire loan within the first few weeks of the term or spending out too much during the holidays when you work more instead of saving it for when you go back to school or when your hours get cut.

Chapter 4: Simplified Financial Planning Goes a Long Way

4.1

Financial planning is ongoing, and it's there to help you make sensible decisions about your money so that you can achieve your life goals. This planning process may involve creating wills to help protect your family, thinking about how the family will live if you aren't making any income, and what they'll do if you fall ill or die. It is okay to spend your money in different ways, but it also helps when you think about all these things as a whole and when you consider a long-term plan. You can come up with your own plan, or you can hire a financial planner if you really have to. The point of minimalist budgets is to save money, so hiring somebody probably isn't something you must do unless you have a lot of assets.

You can come up with a financial plan in
six easy steps:

1. Establish you long- and short-
   term goals.
2. Write out your liabilities and
   assets.
3. Check to see how close you are at
   achieving your goals.
4. Come up with your plan, and
   create a map to reach your goals.
5. Implement that plan, and make
   the needed changes.
6. Review and monitor your plan to
   make adjustments when you need
   to.

It's important that you work out your
life goals and break them down into
long- and short-term goals. Once you do

this, it's important that you prioritize these things and think about how much it is likely to cost you and when you are going to need the money. This is all to make sure you are ready for anything.

4.2

As boring as it may seem, having a financial plan is crucial for seeing the big picture and setting up all of your goals. These are all important parts of mapping out your financial future. When you have a plan, you will find that it is easier for you to make financial decisions and keep yourself on track to meet those goals.

Now, the point of this book and following a minimalist budget is to be able to do it on your own. There are some people, though, that may already have a certified financial planner that can help them. They *can* help, especially if:

- You have an immediate need or an unexpected life event.

- You don't have the knowledge in certain areas like retirement, investments, taxes, or insurance planning.

- You are looking for a professional opinion about a plan that you came up on your own.

- You don't have the time to do your own planning.

- You are trying to improve how to

manage your finances but can't figure out where to start.

Unless you already have one, or you really can't figure out your finances, there is no need to go out and hire a financial planner.

4.3

Through good and bad, thick and thin, those who are successful and coming up with goals and achieving them, at least in finances, are the people who come up with a financial plan and follow through with it. If you are interested in financial security, having a good plan is the way to do it.

The following are eight steps to make sure that you do just that:

1. Figure Out Where Your Money Goes

Once you have taken a look at your finances and figure out where you are like you did in the last chapter, the next thing you have to do is think of where you are going to spend your money now.

To get started with this, carry around a small notebook that will fit in your pocket or purse. Each time you buy something, write down what it is and how much. At the end of your first week, spend some time going over these notes and categorize them. How much has been spent on food?

Transportation? Utilities? Mortgage? Rent? Healthcare? Entertainment? Clothing? Housing? At the end of the first month, consolidate these notes. At the end of the second month, consolidate again. And then at the three-month mark, add all of your expenses up, and devote a little bit of study time.

This process is done to get a picture of what you spend money on and not necessarily cutting things out at this point. This will help you have an idea of the things you need and don't need.

2. Set Your Financial Goals

I want you to ask yourself,

"Where do I see myself in 20 years?" Stay away from generic things like, "I want to be rich." Give a more specific answer: "I want a house with a mortgage that is almost paid off, and an investment portfolio of $400,000, plus a decent sized savings account for emergency expenses."

Make sure you are realistic when you set these goals, and try to be specific. Your goal is to succeed, not to fail. This can only be done if you start with attainable and specific goals.

3. Prepare for the Unexpected with Insurance

If you don't have a family, think about getting some disability insurance to protect your earnings. If you do have a family, think about some disability coverage as well as a lot of life insurance to help protect your loved ones. Make sure you have adequate renters or homeowner's insurance, auto coverage, and health insurance. No matter how your finances may look like, making sure that you are prepared for the unexpected will help you stay on track if something comes up.

4. Watch Your Credit Score

It's important to know your credit score. Once a year, check your

score with the three biggies.
Credit Karma is a great website to
get your TransUnion and
Experian scores. Make sure that
your report doesn't have any
discrepancies. Dispute any errors
that you may see.

5. Begin Saving

The key to any budget and
financial plan is savings, and the
money you spend plays a big part
in this. Even people with large
incomes need to pay attention to
what they spend because they can
easily spend too much. But if you
make sure to control your outgo,
it won't matter what your income
is because it will always be more
than enough.

This is where you use what you have done in the last chapter. You will start cutting back on the things that you don't need from your expenditure. This money that you free up must be put into a savings account. It's a good idea to try to save up three months' worth of income just in case of an emergency. If you do have to use some of this, make sure you replace it.

6. Start to Build a Portfolio

After you have created your emergency fund, you need to look at investing some of your extra cash. For new and experienced investors, one of the easiest things to do is to build a portfolio with mutual funds. You can easily finance mutual funds that match up with your risk tolerance. They also spread your investment risk. Mutual funds will also provide you with professional money management, which is a great idea if you don't have the expertise or time to do this alone.

7. Keep an Eye on Your Plan

It's important that you manage your financial plan to make sure that it stays congruent with your situation. Have any of your goals changed? How does your health, family needs, debt, and income look? How are your investments doing? More importantly, have they done what you've expected?

Depending on your circumstances, it may make sense to look over your plan semi-annually or quarterly. If you check your plan multiple times a year, make sure you don't confuse your long-term and short-term goals.

8. Create an Exit Strategy

You need an exit strategy that matches with your financial goals. If your plan is to purchase a 10,000-square foot home in ten years, you will need to free some of your portfolios up at that point in order to accomplish that goal. Similarly, if you planned on needing college money for your children, you may want an exit strategy for that as well. You will also need to come up with an exit strategy for yourself when you retire and a plan for your heirs.

9. Identify and Evaluate Alternative Course of Action

Coming up with alternatives is important for making the best decisions. There are lots of different factors that will influence your available alternatives; possible courses of action will typically fall into one of these categories:

- Continue your current course of action.
- Expand what your current

situation is.

- Change what your current situation is.
- Pick a different course of action.

Not every single one of these categories will be applicable to each of your decision situations. However, they do show you all of your possible courses of action. Having creativity in your decision-making process is crucial in coming up with effective choices. Considering all of your possible alternatives is going to help you make the best and most satisfying decisions.

When you do decide to pick a different course of action, you will need to evaluate the said course. Things you will have to take into consideration are current economic conditions, personal values, and your life situation.

You need to look at the consequences of choices. All of your decisions will close off a different choice. For example, choosing to invest some money in a stock can mean that you aren't able to take a vacation. Choosing to go to school full time may mean that you will not be able to work full time. Opportunity cost is the amount that you will be giving up when you make a choice. This cost, which is often called a trade-off of a decision, won't always be able to be measured in dollars.

Decision making is going to always be a part of your financial and personal situation. Thus, you are going to have to consider the lost opportunities that are going to result from the decisions you make.

Uncertainty is going to be a part of all of your decisions. Choosing a career field and picking a major at college will all involve some sort of risk. What if you discover that you don't like working in that particular field or that you're not able to find any employment? There are other decisions that involve a lower degree of risk, like putting money into your savings account or buying items that cost just a couple of bucks. The odds of you losing something of great value are very low in these types of situations.

In many different financial decisions, evaluating and identifying risk is pretty hard. The best way for you to consider risk is to get all of the information for it based on your experience and the experiences of other people, and then use financial planning information sources.

Relevant information is needed at every single stage of your decision-making process. Changing economic, social, and personal conditions will require

that you are always
supplementing and updating your
knowledge.

10. Create a Will

Your financial planning doesn't
just end when you die. You have
to make sure that you make
provisions for what is going to
happen to your estate once you
are gone. At the very least, if you
don't have a will written up, your
survivors will probably end up in
probate court working out some
type of deal to distribute all of
your assets.

At the worst, the assets may end
up disappearing into some black
hole. This is the reason why

having a properly executed and drawn will is extremely important. This is literally your financial decision with regards to your state of financial affairs.

It's important that you make some time to meet up with your trusted attorney, and then create a will that will be distributed to your estate according to your wishes. You can come up with it now in one way, and then you can make modifications later on when your financial situations change. You may end up being surprised to discover that you are able to find some sort of peace after you have completed your will. That peace comes from the fact that you will know that you have done all that you can in order to take care of your loved ones once you are gone.

Your Quick Start Action Step:

Now, everything we have covered in this chapter can seem a bit daunting, and it may not be clear as to what you can do right now. We're going to look at ten basic steps that you can take now to help you get started.

1. **What are the motives behind your financial choices?**

   Before you come up with your budget and start to make cuts, you need to figure out what you value the most in your life.

2. **Get yourself organized.**

   Make sure that you have all your
   financial statements in one place
   where you can easily access them.

3. **Make sure that you know
   exactly where all of your
   money goes.**

   I've said this before, and it will
   probably be mentioned in this
   book for several times—it is
   extremely important that you
   know where your money is going.

4. **Shop in a smarter way.**

   Try to make smart shopping

choices to find money without needing to make more.

5. **Look over your debts and reduce them.**

Figure out all of your debts, and use this book to get them paid off.

6. **Create a stronger credit report.**

Keeping a strong credit report will help you easily accomplish your financial goals.

7. **Save money for your future life.**

Make sure that you pay yourself first in order to save up money

and to start your strong
retirement plan.

8. **Set up your financial goals.**

Keep track of all of your goals,
and celebrate your milestones so
that you can reach your dreams
faster.

9. **Come up with a spending
plan.**

Use your spending plan to make
sure that your daily spending
habits don't end up
overwhelming your goals.

10. **Invest your money in order
to reach your goals.**

You can watch your money grow by investing some of the extra so that you can reach your longer-term objectives.

Chapter 5: Unnecessary Compulsive Spending and How to Fix It

5.1

One person's trash is another person's treasure. What may be right for me may not be for you. But I believe that everybody can agree that we all spend money on unnecessary and impractical things that aren't satisfying.

When you don't plan out your big dream, it becomes easy to get distracted by shiny things. Instead of coming up with your life and spending habits to coincide with your real dream, you will continue to work at a place that leaves you with very little free time, and you will spend your money on things you don't need to fill that void. Or you can be interested in buying your own home, but you spend money on things to decorate what you are currently living in to make it feel like the home you want.

Everybody does things that they don't realize until much later. The decision you make right now to get yourself out of debt and saving up money is going to open up doors and spark lots of thoughts that you probably don't have any idea about right now.

5.2

Compulsive spending and shopping can be caused by financial, family, occupational, and interpersonal problems in your life. Some people have such a problem with overspending—and sometimes, it can get to the point of an addiction.

Issues in relationships may happen

because of excessive spending, and your efforts to cover up these debts and purchases will only make things worse. People who engage in this kind of shopping may end up becoming pre-occupied with their behavior and can learn how to spend less with some help and time. You may even start to experience anxiety or depression because of your shopping or spending, which can end up affecting your school or work performance.

You may experience financial problems if the money you use is borrowed or if there is excessive use of credit to make your compulsive purchases. Most of the time, the extent of damage you have created only gets discovered once you have accumulated a large sum of debt that will cause the need for a drastic change in your life to fix it.

5·3

If you're tired of compulsive shopping and overspending, then there are several things you can do to overcome this issue.

1. **Do some inventory**

   It's common for people to purchase new stuff just because they can't see the things they already have. Weed out your clothing and get rid of unmatched, ill-fitting, or well-worn ones. This is also true for knickknacks, household products, and tools.

2. Buy good-quality products

This may seem counterintuitive, but it's common for people to never use things that they love and that gives them great pleasure. This is often due to their want to protect it because they love it so much. Instead, they also buy a cheap knockoff to use. Get the good stuff that you love and actually use it, so you don't have to buy a cheaper alternative.

3. Get rid of temptation

Think about having a friend that is constantly telling you about these amazing deals or that you have to try the new pizza place.

When you hear these things, it puts you in a place to consider these purchases that you probably won't have thought about.

4. Wait it out

When you really want to buy something, think about it for about 20 minutes. After you have let your head clear, reconsider how and when you will actually use it. Instead of deciding whether or not to get it, give yourself a chance to think of something that you may need instead. Typically, these impulse purchases will seem less urgent after you sleep on them.

5. Remember, it's fine not to buy

Shopping takes time, and it can end up making you feel like you wasted a lot of time if you don't buy anything. Outlet malls are typically a dangerous place for those who are trying to reduce their consumption. It's common that people will buy things they don't need instead of leaving the store empty-handed so that it doesn't feel like the trip is wasted.

6. Pay with Cash

People will normally end up spending a lot more money when they pay with debit cards or credit cards. When you charge items, you will feel more disconnected from your money. You don't see them as dollars.

Spending becomes a lot more real when you have to take the money out of your wallet or purse. This is why it is best that you immediately set money aside from your paycheck for bills, and then take the remaining out in cash. This will make you a lot less likely to go on a compulsive shopping binge because you will have a very limited amount of money to spend.

7. Fill Up your Life with Social Connections

Most of the time, when a person compulsively spends, they are trying to fill their needs by making connections with other people through their shopping. The problem is, they aren't able to ever completely fill in that void.

That's why it is a good idea to fill up your life with other social activities and connections. These things may include book clubs, charities, sports clubs, and the like.

Shopping is so often caused by not having as much of a social life—but if instead of shopping, you fill up your days with other things, there will be two things that happen. You will find that you don't wind up at the mall as often, and you will be hanging around with people who don't always go shopping. When you hang around with other shoppers, you will only get more encouragement from them to buy things.

This is very similar to the rationale behind alcoholics not going to bars. It becomes a lot easier to not make purchases when you aren't being forced to say no to yourself.

Your Quick Start Action Step

The hardest aspect of personal finances

is trying to figure out the best way to use your money. It is hard trying to figure out ways to save a lot of money on a tiny budget. The main way to lessen your spending is by cutting back a bit in every area. It may take some work, but you will find your stress begin to go down when you are about to pay off some of your debt. Here are some ways to help you cut back:

- Put all your bonuses into a savings account. It's a great feeling when you change your purse and find a $20 bill. Don't put it in your pocket—rather, pay yourself by putting it into your savings account.

- Cook at home. It's hard to have the time and energy to make a home-cooked meal when you get home from work. Begin cooking twice a week, and slowly increase it one day every week until you are cooking every night. If this isn't realistic for you, take time on the weekend to meal prep some dinners for the week ahead. By doing this, you will have meals ready when you get home. This goes for morning coffee, too. Buying that large specialty coffee each day can add up to a lot of money. Take the time to brew some coffee at home before you leave for work.

- Write down the things you need from the store before you go. If you have ever gone to the store without a list or when hungry, it is tempting to buy more food than normal. Preplan your meals and buy what you need in one trip so that you don't spend money on items you don't need and that you don't forget what you do need. Lists will ensure that you don't have to make another trip to the store and that you aren't faced with temptation.

- Make a shopping limit. Don't buy things on impulse. If you want an expensive coat that you really don't need, wait a few days to see if you are still thinking about it. This lets you check online to find a cheaper alternative.

- Cancel memberships, and cut your entertainment bill. It may be easy to forget about recurring monthly bills. If you have a gym membership that you don't use, it is time to cancel it. If you have a Netflix membership but never use it, cancel it. Getting rid of extra expenses can make a big difference to your budget.

- Learn to love DIY projects. Don't go to a spa to have a facial; make one for yourself. Pinterest has many useful tools for those of you who have the guts to try it. You can find recipes, cleaning hacks, and ways to use things around your house.

- Use an app to help you budget. It is easy to overspend when you don't set limits for yourself. Apps like Quicken and Mint can help you track monthly, weekly, and daily spending so that you can see where you must cut back and so that you can get advice for your financial goals and needs.

Chapter 6: Dealing with Debt

6.1

The simplest way to describe debt is money that is owed from one party to the other. It may get complicated quickly. It all depends on the amount of debt you have and the way you handle it. Debt can be a useful tool or baggage that complicates your life.

Knowing the right way to handle debt can be difficult especially if you constantly struggle to cover your monthly bills. There are various ways to handle each type of debt. There are also ways to get relief from debt. Just be careful of companies that sound too good to be true or promise you absurd things. Here are the two most common types of debt and ways to handle them:

- **Secured debt**: A secured debt is one where the borrower has provided some asset as collateral to secure the loan. Mortgages and car loans are examples of a secured debt. If you don't pay, the creditor can take the said asset like foreclosing your house or repossessing your car.

- **Unsecured debt** is never backed by an asset. One example is a credit card. This doesn't mean you won't have consequences if you don't pay your bills. The creditor can sell your debt to a collection agency that will then call you night and day for payment. If you still don't pay, they might be able to sue you for payment. This might lead to

your wages being garnished.
Some creditors might sue you
without using a collection agency.

6.2

Most people wonder how much of their
money is theirs and the amount they pay
toward debt factors in on how their debt
is accumulated. There are many reasons
why we have debt, such as
unemployment or unforeseen
emergencies. More often than not, debt
is caused by bad spending habits. If you
aren't paying with cash, it will cost you
to spend money.

Think about a credit card being
somebody who is granting you a favor to
buy things you cannot afford but will let
you pay them off later. Actually, the

truth is you just wind up owing more and not getting everything you need.

Everybody alive tries to keep up with their neighbors. They have the life we've always wished for, and we will never be able to keep up with them. These things we long for lead us to huge amounts of debt. When we don't know how to manage this debt, it can cause our credit card bills to grow endlessly.

Let's look at making a purchase of $500 without a credit card. You think this is a good deal because you only have to pay $15 a month. This is very manageable for you. What you don't realize is the creditor is adding an additional $147 to that bill for interest. If you only pay $15 each month, it is going to take you four years to pay off that $500 charge. That is assuming you have an interest rate of 14.7 percent. If your credit card has a higher interest rate, this purchase at 22 percent means you are going to be paying out an additional $280 in interest. Yes, you still have those four years to pay off a total of $780, so is that item worth that much more?

If you add in all our wants with the large investments of cars and homes along with the planned necessities like weddings and college as well as the unplanned emergencies like relocation, unemployment, and medical emergencies, it is easy to visualize how quickly debt can grow. The main reason people get into debt is a combination of personal and impersonal finances.

6.3

Even if your debt is small, you have to manage it well. You have to make your payments on time and be sure it doesn't get out of hand. If your debt is large, you must put in more effort to pay it off while making your other payments.

1. **Know your creditors and the amounts you owe.**

   Create a list of debts that include the creditor, complete amount you owe, how much your payments are, and when they are due. Use a credit report to confirm your debts. Having the debts in front of you lets you see the bigger picture, so you are aware of your whole debt. Don't make a list and then forget about it. Look at it from time to time, especially when you pay your bills. Update the list every month or two when the list changes.

2. Pay your dues on time.

Making late payments will make it harder for you to pay off the debt because you are going to have to pay an extra late fee for each payment you miss. If you miss two payments, your finance charges and interest rate will go up. If you use a calendar, place your payments and set an alarm to give you an alert a couple days before the payment needs to be made. If you miss a payment, don't wait until it becomes due again. The creditor may report it

to a credit bureau. Make your
payment once you remember.

3. Make a bill-paying calendar.

Use a calendar to help you figure
out what bill to pay with a certain
paycheck. Write every bill's
payment on the day it is due.
Next, put in the calendar when
you get paid. If you get paid on
the same date, this is an easy step
for you. If your paychecks come
on a different day, it will help to
make a note each month.

4. Always make your minimum payment.

If the minimum amount is all you
can pay, that is fine—just do it on

time. This isn't going to get you any progress in paying off your debt. It will keep the debt from growing and will keep your account good. If you miss a payment, it becomes harder to get caught up. Your account may go into default.

5. **Figure out what debt you need to pay off fastest.**

Paying off any credit card debt first is the best strategy since these have higher interest rates. It must be the priority since it will cost you the most money. Use your list of debts, and rank them in order that you want to pay them off. You may also choose to pay off the one with the lowest balance first.

6. **Pay off any charge-offs and collections.**

    You can only pay what you can afford. If you have limited funds to repay debts, try to focus on keeping other accounts in good standing. Never sacrifice good accounts for ones that have already changed your credit. Pay the past due accounts when you can afford them. These creditors are going to keep hounding you for payment until it is brought current.

7. **Have an emergency fund to help out in hard situations.**

You may have to go into debt to cover an emergency if you don't want to dip into your savings account. A small emergency fund can cover small expenses that may pop up now and then. Begin by working to create a small fund. An amount of $ 1,000 is a great place to start. When you have that amount, try to increase it to another thousand. You want to try to create a reserve that equals your six months' pay.

8. Create a monthly budget to plan expenses.

Keeping a budget will help you make sure that you have the money to cover all expenses each month. Plan in advance so that you can take action if you are going to be short one month. Budgets help you plan how to use any extra money you may have left after all expenses have been paid. You may have enough money to pay another debt off.

9. See the signs that you are in need of help.

If you see that it is too hard for you to pay your bills and debts every month, you can turn to a debt relief company for help. Check out credit counseling agencies in your area. Other options are bankruptcy, debt settlement, and debt consolidation. All of these have disadvantages and advantages, so check each option carefully. If you have a spending problem, you can seek help through a Debtors Anonymous group. This is similar to Alcoholics Anonymous.

10. Change Your Debt Like Behaviors

In order to get out of debt, you have to eliminate the reasons you may up in debt in the first place. Even winning the PowerBall Jackpot won't fix your problem if you don't learn how to spend less than what you make.

Everybody has their own reasons for winding up in debt. Medical bills, job loss, school, or just plain young stupidity are all widely common reasons. However, the reason you have gotten into debt doesn't matter all that much. What matters the most is that you don't let this happen again. Here are some things you must not do:

- If you have to take out $50k in student loans to get your bachelor's degree, don't take out an extra $100k for a Ph.D.

- Did you end up falling into a large pile of debt when you lost your job? Resolve, after you have gotten out of debt, to work on building up an emergency fund so that you won't have to face this problem again.

- If you spend several years living a life that you can't afford, then you have to figure out the life that you can actually afford, and get to that point.

That last point is a lot easier said than done. The truth is that the last point is the main reason for this book and about a third of all financial articles you can find online. Let's be honest: how many articles have you seen that are labeled, "Live within your means," "Spend less than your monthly income," and so on? Why has there been so much stuff written on this very simple concept?

This is because after a person has gotten used to living in a certain way, it is extremely hard to change that habit. It will be like having to live on ramen after living for two years on The Capital Grille.

11. When to Refinance or Consolidate

Two of the most common things people do when faced with a lot of debt is consolidation and refinancing. Consolidation means that you put all of your debts into one loan. This will help you by allowing you to deal with only one lender. This means you won't be faced with several different monthly billing statements.

Refinancing means that you replace all of your old debts with a new loan. The goal of doing this is to get a lower interest rate. The majority of students will use consolidation for their student loans. This works if all of the debts are from a government program.

There are many different online calculators to help you figure out if refinancing works for you and to make sure that you pick the best one. Before you decide to consolidate or refinance, take the following into consideration:

- Has your credit score gone up

any? This will place you in a favorable light with lenders. This means you will be able to start a tangible process of removing all of your old debt with a new lender that offer better terms.

- Do you already have low-interest rates? If this is the case, you can take advantage of it. Change your variable rate to a fixed rate.

- Are you able to change your payment terms? Dragging your debt along with you for a long time won't help you to become debt-free. If you are making more money and can afford it, start making larger payments each month.

Your Quick Start Action Step:

You are not alone in your debt. Most people in the world are also in debt. If you live in denial, it will only increase your money problems along with your anxiety. When you can face your situation, paying off those debts may be easier than you realize.

- Fast facts: The first thing you have to do is to figure out how big your problem is. Start by looking at your last bank statement and finding any missing paperwork. Open bills you have been neglecting. Create a list of the amount you owe every company and their interest rates. When you have figured out this information, you will begin to prioritize all your debts.

- Transfer to a zero-percent credit card. If you have expensive credit cards, see if you can transfer the debt to a zero-percent credit card. These cards can eliminate interest charges for a certain period. This makes sure that every cent you repay will go toward paying down your balance. In order to get the most out of these cards, you need to pay off the balance in the offer window. If you know you can't repay the whole amount in the introductory period, look for low-interest rate cards. You are still going to pay interest every month, but it will be at a low rate. These types of cards require an unblemished credit score.

- Think about overdraft options. If you pay a lot of interest in overdraft fees, this can quickly accelerate your debt problems. If you think you may be paying too much for your overdraft service, see if your bank has a different account you can switch to, or drop the overdraft from your account entirely.

- You may consider a personal loan. There may be a time when getting a personal loan can help you manage your debt. Find a leading market rate with the APR lower than what you are currently paying on your credit card. If you look around, it may be possible to find a rate lower than eight percent. This is a lot better than the normal 17 to 22 percent that normal credit cards charge. If you need to borrow a large sum of money, a personal loan is a way to go. Larger loans usually come with lower APRs than those with smaller amounts. Don't borrow more money than you need since this may increase your chances of getting deeper into debt. Always shop around. You aren't going to get a good rate if you accept the first offer from the first lender you go to.

Chapter 7:
Overall Budget Techniques Applied to Daily, Monthly, and Long-Term Expenses

say NO
have fun
love
relax
breath
smile
be happy
unplug
meditate
reach out
rest
enjoy
take a nap
love
smile
have fun
slow
let it go
take it easy
relax
be positive
down
laugh
seize the day
go outside
stay calm
simplify
prioritize
eliminate
reduce stress
exercise
love
enjoy life
declutter

7.1

We've used the word budget and budgeting a lot throughout this book. While it may sound like a bad word to many, especially for those who know how taking a deeper look at their finances is going to reveal some pretty bad habits that they would rather stay hidden, it is an extremely helpful tool when it comes to a minimalist budget.

Budgeting is known to be difficult, even when it comes to just keeping track of where all of your money goes. The first question people will ask you is if you are trying to budget before taxes (i.e. gross income) or after taxes (i.e. net income)?

If you want to begin with your gross income, it will be best to look at the percentage that is saved in your 401(k). If your company offers you a match offer, make sure you put away enough to get it. The maximum contribution of an employee for a 401(k) is $18,000 in 2016, so try not to go over this limit. However, this does not include what your employer will contribute. The limit for you and your employer's contribution is $53,000. You can also have health insurance premiums that are automatically deducted from your pay if your company provides you insurance, so there is a chance that you won't have to include this into your post-tax budget.

After you have become comfortable with how your payroll and pre-tax deduction saving works, you can then focus on your budget for net income, which is what most people look at day-to-day. If you plan on being really minimalist with your budget, here is a suggestion: the 65-25-10 rule.

- 65% is spent on your day-to-day living.
- 25% is spent on large expenses and retirement, including emergencies.
- 10% is given away to your favorite causes or charity.

You can get really nitty-gritty about it, and break them down even further. However, when you are trying to see the big picture, sometimes it's good just to have a few numbers. If you have to provide your own savings, then you may want the breakdown to be 65-15-10-10.

- 65% is still day-to-day expenses.
- 15% is your emergency and large expenses.
- 10% is retirement expenses.
- 10% is charity expenses.

The hard decisions are made in the day-to-day expenses. If you make sure that you automate your savings money and set them aside, you will make sure that you won't spend the amount that you intended to save on eating out or impulse buys because the money won't be in your checking account.

When you are first starting out with budgeting, or when you are trying to get a handle on your spending, try using a cash-only method or limit yourself a lot when it comes to using your credit card. If you do use a credit card, start going in and manually categorizing and entering your purchases so that you will become aware of the things you are spending.

Much like how you log your calories when you want to lose weight, typing in each dollar you spend into a spreadsheet will help you to become more aware of the way you use your money, which is the first step you need to take toward financial success.

After you have gotten a handle on your spending, you can upgrade to a program that will download your credit card and bank information so that you won't have to write everything down by hand, but make sure that you still set aside some time to really look over your weekly spending so that you can see how you are balancing yourself across different categories. If you overspend in one category, that's okay—just try to under-spend in another one.

This budgeting will require a bit of work on your part—but in the end, it will help you save for and spend on the things that are the most important.

7.2

Even though it is extremely important and significant, financial education isn't something that is normally taught in our educational system. The skills to budget and the ability to stick to a said budget are elusive skills to most. However, it is crucial that you develop these skills because it guarantees your material survival.

Since there is a lack of financial knowledge in the consumer society, there are two major problems that must be faced:

1. Downsizing but not sacrificing on the fun things; and
2. Controlling finances while coming up with a budget.

Based on minimalism principles, it helps to outline some basic rules while providing you with many different ways to curb frivolous spending and to save money. When you figure out what you need, you will be able to live a lifestyle that is more manageable.

Everybody can benefit from living a simpler life. Minimalism not only helps your mental and physical health, but it is also able to improve your financial health. There are several straightforward methods to help you keep your finances on track:

- Improve spending habits – Start incorporating a minimalist approach to your finances, and stay away from becoming a compulsive consumerist. You control your spending habits through learning the psychological traps that end up causing overspending.

- Feel financially secure – You learn budgeting methods, such as fixed-amount budgeting, ratio-based, and A-Z. Make use of a budgeting software program, and create a solid savings strategy to

help get you out of debt and get
yourself ready for retirement.

- Stop hating your finances.
  Improve your self-confidence
  with budgeting tips and learn
  smart financial goals.

Your financial health directly indicates
your overall health. That means that it is
crucial to truly evaluate your finances
and improve your relationship with
money. As scary as this may seem,
downsizing can positively affect your
wellbeing, financially and physically.
Minimalism will teach you that you
don't actually need as much as you
believe you do. Less really is more.
Instead of constantly shuffling to keep
up with a lifestyle of spending, spend
less and then only spend on the things

that you really need. Save up your money so that you can invest in your future.

Money management is an important skill for everybody that consumes or earns. Regardless of how large your income is, you can still budget, increase your self-worth, and save money.

Once you have learned how to budget your money, you will be able to clearly see the areas where your money is going, when you get it, and where you can save. This will not only help you reduce your debts, but you will then have bigger savings for those larger expenses, such as a vacation or a car. This means that budgeting is a lifestyle change, and a minimalist budget can completely change your life.

Reading this book is going to be a lot different from actually applying the things that you have learned. You can take notes and mark pages, but once you put this down, you can end up forgetting everything you're supposed to do. That's where the how and action steps come into play.

7.3

Having a budget means more than just getting your bills paid on time. Having a budget involves figuring out how much you must spend and on what. The 50/20/30 budget provides you with a proportional guide to keep your spending aligned with your savings goals.

Adults, especially those that are just starting out, are able to benefit by following along with this simple principle. Once you know the best way to achieve a balanced budget, you are then able to take the next steps to further customize the budget around your own needs.

This 50/20/30 rule is able to help those twenty-somethings begin to sort out the complicated world of finances. It's important that you make an effort to get yourself into a habit—and when you do that, budgeting will become a lot easier in your life. Sure, you are able to make a few tweaks here and there, but try to stay close to the core of this concept. This way, you are guaranteed to gain financial ground instead of losing it.

Before you do anything else, you need to figure out your monthly net income. This is the amount of money that you bring home at the end of each month. There are a lot of people that have deductions taken from their check, which includes medical insurance, HSA funding, and retirement contributions. You can base your budget on the money you actually receive, or you can add these things back in. Either way is going to work, but I think you will get a better picture if you add these numbers back in.

Let's say that after deductions, you bring home $4,000 a month. The deductions are currently $800 for insurances, $100 for HAS, and $600 for 401(k). Adding those back in, your true take-home will be $5,500.

You will place this amount at the top of your spreadsheet, and this is what you base your budget on.

50% of your income must go to essentials.

To start following this rule, set aside half of your income, and no more, for the absolute necessities for living. This may sound like a pretty large percentage, but when you start to consider everything that belongs in this category, it will make more sense.

So that you are completely clear, essential expenses are the things that you will almost certainly have to pay— no matter where you live, where you work, or what your future plans are. In general, these types of expenses are pretty much the same for everybody and will include utility bills, transportation costs, food expenses, and rent/housing amortization. This percentage amount will allow you to adjust it while also maintaining a balanced and sound budget. Keep in mind that this is more about the total sum than it is about each individual cost. For instance, there are some that live in high-rent areas, but they can walk to work; others have cheaper housing, but the transportation is more expensive.

Figuring out how much you absolutely need to live each month is critical to creating your budget. It is best if you look at your last few months of spending to make sure that you get an accurate picture. Make sure that you don't estimate. Trust me—you will not get it right. Everybody pretty much will underestimate the amount of money they spend. For example, most people will not want to admit how much they actually spend on dining out.

Remember: this section includes everything you need to have in order to keep your life going.

The hardest part here is to separate the wants from the needs. You may be needing some new clothes, but that doesn't mean you need to buy them from Niemen Marcus.

Some people need to have an internet connection at home for school or work, but there are some people for whom it is a luxury.

It is important that you are honest with yourself with what you truly need and the things that you don't.

With the income example from above, 50% of your income will be $2,750. Let's say then that you have a fixed expense and items with a set payment that may look like this:

- $100 credit card payment
- $250 car payment
- $350 utility payment
- $600 insurance payment
- $800 rent payment

Then, you have your semi-discretionary items, which are items that will vary each month:

- $25 for basic clothing

- $225 for gas
- $400 for groceries

Depending on your lifestyle, you may also have expenses such as child-related expenses, as well as home or vehicle maintenance.

Your total needs then come out to be $2,750. Depending on your actual situation, you may find that you will have to allocate more of your budget to your essentials. This is okay especially when you are just getting your finances under control. Plus, these numbers are perfect world numbers. There aren't going to be too many people who will have these types of numbers.

The point of this is you have to work on your budget until you are actually about to make these percentages work. You will probably have to pay off debt when you first start. Once that's taken care of, you will have more money to use elsewhere.

20% of your income must go to savings.

The next thing you need to do is to dedicate 20 percent of your take-home pay to savings. This must include rainy-day funds, debt payments, and savings plans. These are things that need to be added but will not endanger your living or cause you to end up homeless if you don't. That may seem like an oversimplification, but hopefully, you understand what I mean. You must only pay this category once you have taken care of your essentials and before you even start thinking about your personal spending.

This must be viewed as your "get ahead" category. The portion of 50% or less is the goal for your essentials, while 20% or more needs to be the goal of this section. This will mean that you can pay off debt quicker, and you will make more significant strides toward a stress-free future by devoting as much of your money as you safely can to this area.

The word retirement probably doesn't seem that important at the age of 24, but it will become even more pressing in the decades to come. Keep in mind that there is a large advantage in starting early especially when it comes to compounded interests and letting your funds grow.

With the previous example, you have $1,100 for this category. Depending on your actual situation, here are a few recommendations for this:

- If you are in debt and working to pay it off, I recommend creating an emergency fund of $1,000, and then use the remaining money to pay off your debt.

- After you have gotten yourself out of debt, I recommend coming up with a larger emergency fund, which will be worth three to six months of essential expenses.

- After your debt has been paid off and you have created your emergency fund, your full 20% can go into savings—and it will be the best feeling in the world.

Saving up your money is one of the most important things you can do for financial success. After you have learned how to delay the gratification and after you are able to place yourself first in your spending equations, you will find that it is easier to get ahead.

30% of your income goes to personal expenses.

This is the last category and the one that will make the biggest difference when it comes to your budget. These are unnecessary expenses that enhance your life. There are a lot of financial experts that see this as completely discretionary, but modern society has caused many of these luxuries to become more mandatory. This will all depend on the things that you want in life and the things that you are willing to sacrifice on. The main reason why this section is larger than the savings section is that there are a lot of things that go in it.

These expenses include things like coffee shop trips, cable bill, and cell phone plan. If you work on-the-go or travel a lot for work, a cell phone plan will become more of a necessity instead of a luxury. However, there is a bit of wiggle room since you can choose your service tier. Other things that fall into this category are dining out, weekend trips, and gym memberships. Only you are able to choose which expenses are personal, and which you are obligated to pay for. Similar to the way the 50% must go toward essentials, the 30% is the maximum amount that you can allow to go towards personal expenses. The less you spend in this section, the more you will be able to pay down your debts and secure your future.

Continuing with the financial example, you have $1,650 to spend on this category. Everybody's wants are going to vary, but the main goal is to make sure that you don't dip into your savings money.

Establishing these good habits will last you a lifetime. You don't have to make thousands of dollars a week for this to work; anybody is able to follow this. Since this is percentage-based, you can apply the same proportion whether you have an entry-level salary, or if you are already years into your career.

A word of caution: it's important that you don't take this too literally. Everybody's life is a little bit different. This plan is here to provide you with a framework that you can work with. After you have reviewed your expenses and income, you have to figure out what's essential and what isn't. Then you can come up with a budget that will help you use your money more efficiently. Years later, you will be able to fall back on these guidelines so that your budget can evolve with your life.

A good software to look at is Mint, and it makes it easy to live by this budget. Once you have spent some time figuring out which expense fall into what section, you will be able to come up with your first budget and keep yourself on track.

Your situation will change, and Mint will allow you to be able to adjust things when this happens.

Your Quick Start Action Step:

While the 50/20/30 budget is your goal, you're probably looking for something you can do right now or something you can see results in quickly. While what you must do right now is sit down to look at your spending, there are some other things that will help with your minimalist budget.

1. **Clean up**

    When your surroundings and senses are dominated by furniture and clothing, you will lose your ability to appreciate the things you have. Try using a vacuum cleaner, wiping up dust, and clearing out the trash—anything that you can do on a regular basis. Keeping a neat household will give you the ability to appreciate the things that you have bought—your chair, desk, bed, cooking wares, and so on will be easier seen once the clutter is gone.

2. **Take inventory, figure out the need, and donate**

While you are cleaning up, think about the things that you actually need and what things are beneficial to you. If you find clothing that you haven't worn in the past year, maybe you can donate it. Do you have electronics or shoes that have been shoved in the corner for a rainy day? How often are you going to use it? What value does it bring? Also, if you need this motivation, donations will also give you a tax break.

3. Create your budget

The time has come to bite the bullet, sit down, and come up with that budget. The only way a minimalist budget is going to help you is if you actually sit down and do it. Figure out your wants and needs and the money you bring in each month, and make that your starting point.

Chapter 8: Recycling the Right Way While Still Making Money

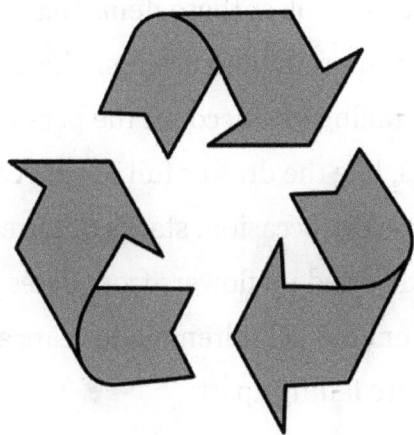

8.1

Everybody has those closets, drawers, cabinets, and possibly rooms filled with things we just can't think about throwing away. We can't even get the energy to look at these items that may be both important and useless. This isn't even taking into account the personal items, like the drawer full of past cards from every occasion, stacks of unread books, dried up flowers from dates years ago, or crafts children made years ago that are falling apart.

There is no reason to hang onto paychecks, paid bills, contracts, or manuals from appliances that have been dead for years. All these stuff will weigh you down and will take up needed space. It will create emotional baggage and drama.

Once you begin throwing out old stuff like those manuals, contracts, paid bills, and paychecks, start crossing off things on that to-do list like running marathons or swimming the English Channel.

Decluttering isn't about just cleaning out your closet and desk. It's about getting rid of all the things you keep hanging onto from the past like unfinished business, relationships, and careers. It will be a big moment of power in your life.

Behind all that clutter is a thousand reasons why we hang onto things. You may read that stack of books one day. You may lose that weight and finally get back into those pants that have been in your closet since your college days. These items don't motivate us—they just fill us with shame and guilt. We *hope* we can one day read those books or fit into those clothes. When we don't, we begin to feel guilty. How much of one thing do you need to remind you of that moment in time? How many things must you hang onto until it begins to control your life?

We hold onto things thinking that we are going to need them. It is easy hiding things you don't need or use in a cabinet or closet. These things are going to pile up to a point where you won't be able to ignore them any longer. Even if it is in a closet behind closed doors, you are still hanging onto it. You have to figure out why this item is important instead of just shoving it under a rug.

8.2

Keeping your house clean can be a daunting task. Keeping it clean is important for a lot of reasons. These things can help you have a better life:

- You will do more. If your home gets disorganized or dirty, it may be hard to focus on what you need to do. You may get distracted by surface cleaning or trying to organize things. These will keep you from doing the important things. When your home is organized and clean, you will get more things done and have fewer distractions.

- You will be able to find things. If you are constantly losing your cell phone or keys, a clean house will simplify your life. You won't spend as much time looking for these misplaced items. Go through the mail when you get it. Get rid of papers you don't need or want. You are going to feel better once everything is organized.

- You will feel creative. A clean house lets your mind become creative and feel more relaxed. If you are surrounded by disorganization and uncleanliness, your mind will focus on the chaos, and your creative juices won't flow.

- You will have friends over. There isn't anything more embarrassing than inviting friends over, and your house is in shambles. This can make you stop inviting friends over. Don't let your house stop you from spending time with friends and loved ones. When you keep your home clean, you will invite more people into your home.

- It is good for your children. It isn't good for anybody of any age to live in filth. Young children who crawl are going to pick up everything on the floor and put it into their mouth. Children are susceptible to mildew, mold, and bacteria that can hurt their health. Keep your house sanitized and clean to keep your children healthy.

- You will have better sleep. There isn't a better feeling than jumping into a bed that has clean sheets and telling a clean house good night. You will rest better when you aren't waking up to chaos. Your mind will rest peacefully in a clean house.

8.3

Some stuff is easy to set aside, such as that company t-shirt that has holes in it and is too small or those birthday cards from several years ago. If you still have things like this, stop now and throw them out. Once you can get rid of things that are easy to identify, you can begin

on the rest of the stuff. Let's find out
what needs to stay and what needs to go:

1. **Sort it out:**

    You have to begin by sorting out
    all your excess. Put the items into
    categories that you can go
    through separately. These need to
    include gadgets, cables, clothing,
    and books. You can even be more
    specific if you have a problem
    collecting things for a hobby—
    things like sports equipment,
    photo albums, board games, and
    puzzles. These things can quickly
    accumulate at home. If
    something is taking up too much
    space, you need to find a category
    for it. With every category, sort
    the items into three piles: what

you are keeping, what you are getting rid of, and what you aren't sure about. You have to get ruthless. When did you use that juicer? Are you going to use it later? Do you really need it? After you have sorted them all, go through all the piles you aren't certain about, and try to get rid of half of it. Now, it's time to put everything back. The things you are getting rid of goes into boxes, trash bags, or whatever you have decided to do with them just so they go out of the house. Now, the things you are keeping need to be put away nicely and neatly. Then, take a minute to admire all the new space you have created. Pick up the things you aren't sure about and place them somewhere. If it is clothing that needs hanging, hang it in a separate closet, or put it in a drawer. Don't put it together with what you are keeping. Keep track of what you will and will not use in the next 30 days. If you will use it, put it where it belongs. If you will not, get rid of it after the time limit is up.

2. **Repeat this step.**

Not right now. You have gotten rid of a lot of things you thought you cared about. You aren't in any emotional state to go through a bunch more possessions. Wait another 30 days, and do the process all over again.

There are several options when you want to get rid of stuff. You can donate, sell, or just trash them. Let's look at how you can do each of these things:

- Donating is an easy way to get rid of stuff you don't want. Finding a local Goodwill or Salvation Army are good places to start. There may also be other charities in your area that run thrift stores to help them run their charities such as Brother Wolf or a local animal shelter. You can even have an open house party where you invite your friends for some food and fun, and then they get to go through your stuff and take home things they want.

- Selling is a great way to get rid of your things and make some money, too. The easiest way to start is eBay or Craigslist. Craigslist is great for large items you can't ship like furniture. You may decide to sell all your things through Craigslist, especially if you don't want the hassle of shipping. eBay is great if you have collectibles you want to sell, though.

- Most of the stuff in your house may fit into a hard drive if you put in some effort. If you have old photos or VHS tapes, putting these things on digital hard drives will save you a bunch of money.

- Throwing things out is the easiest of all since you probably already have trash bags on hand. Fill up the bag with things that you can't or don't want to sell, and take it to the curb. Throwing things out isn't easy, but you need to do it safely. Technology doesn't need to go to the landfill. If it can be recycled, take it to a recycler. Check out Gazelle to see if they want your old electronics.

3. **Get rid of unused sports equipment.**

Yes, I completely believe you when you said you were going to use that mini trampoline to jump on every day, and I'm sure you were going to incorporate some amazing workouts with those pretty pink free weights.

Let's be honest with ourselves: none of that actually happened, and now, your cabinets are filled up with retired sporting equipment. When it comes to getting rid of stuff, you have to be completely honest with yourself. Ask, "Am I really going to ever use this stuff?"

4. **"Acquired" mini hotel toiletries.**

Everybody gets excited when they stay at a hotel and see all those little toiletries. Then, you realize you have a box full of travel-size soaps that won't ever get used. Unless you are planning on going camping, or you have a lot of guests who are going to stay with you, these are things that must definitely be gotten rid of.

5. **Throw out things such as bread makers.**

Do you really need that bread maker? All of these clunky machines are just taking up a bunch of important space in your home. They are just gathering dust, and they aren't really necessary. If you do actually make your own bread, you can use your oven and clear out a big spot in your kitchen.

6. Throw out things that you don't ever play.

Did anybody in your household believe they were going to learn how to play the guitar but then lost interest? Has the expensive electric drum kit turned into a clothes hanger?

Learning to get rid of things that you've had full intention of using can be pretty hard—but if you've not actually used it at this point, you probably ever won't. Take that plunge, and get rid of those things to free up some space.

7. **Crazy pizza gadgets**

All of those snazzy pizza makers
and those neat little pizza cutting
shears looked like amazing tools,
and you thought they were a good
idea. But when did you last use
them? Unless you make a pizza
once or more each week, then you
probably don't really need any of
those items taking up space in
your kitchen.

8. **Throw out everything that is
   already broken.**

Why are you still holding onto
things that are broken? If you can
fix the broken items, then fix
them; otherwise, just throw them

away. You can also donate them or sell them to junk shops. There are some artists that will use donated toys to make things, so you can browse through some of the local boards before you throw the items away.

9. **Throw out all of those old cookbooks.**

The old cookbooks may look pretty, but do you really use them all that much? If you don't use them often, then it's probably a good idea to get rid of them. It can be extremely hard to get rid of things that you are fond of, but there are also plenty of online resources for you to use when it comes to finding a new recipe to cook—and these take up much

less space. You can print out your
favorite recipes and then put
them in a three-ring binder. That
way, you have only one cookbook,
and it only has recipes that you
actually cook.

10. **Throw out your old receipts.**

Chances are, if you check your
coat pockets, wallets, or bags—
you are going to find at least one
receipt in them. Let's be honest:
how many times have you pulled
a coat out to wear at the
beginning of winter that you
haven't worn since last winter,
and you stick your hand in the
pocket and pull out a chunk of
receipts and tissues?

Gather them all up, and then glance through them before you get rid of them to make sure that you have accounted for all those things. This may help you realize that you are spending too much money on certain things.

Learning how to throw away things on a regular basis will help you stay more organized and reduce your clutter.

11. Get rid of your old magazines.

Having some magazines around the house for guests is a nice thing, but chances are that you aren't going to read those out-of-date magazines ever again, so it's a good idea to recycle them. You can even try to donate those magazines to local libraries or doctor's offices. Before you allow these things to pile up in your house, see if there is something that you can do with them first.

12. Get rid of your old pillows.

Throwing out things like pillows tend to be rather tricky because they aren't cheap, but you think they are going to last a lifetime. In order to figure out if you need to get a new pillow, try this:

Fold the pillow in half, if it easily stays in this folded position, then you need to get a new pillow.

Your body and hair oils penetrate

the pillow while you sleep, and this will start to change the color of the pillow. It will then become a breeding ground for dust mites and other odor-causing bacteria. You can often donate these old pillows to pet shelters. They will use them for pet beds.

13. Get rid of the jewelry you no longer wear or have never worn.

Go through your jewelry box and see if there are any pieces that you don't wear anymore—worse yet if you have any that you haven't taken out of their box or their packaging. You may find a bunch of jewelry that you don't wear or haven't even worn. You can choose to donate the jewelry, or you can try to sell them and get some extra money put into your savings.

14. Throw out clothes that you don't ever wear.

This is especially true if you are trying to lose weight. Don't hold onto that size-six pair of jeans just in case you are able to fit back in them. Chances are, if you make it back down to that size, you are going to want to buy new clothes instead of wearing old ones. Another great trick is that every time you wear an article of clothing, flip the clothes hanger around so that you know you have worn it recently. Then every six months to a year, go through your closet and get rid of clothes that hanger hasn't been moved.

15. Recycle those old boxes.

You may believe that you are being organized by holding onto those old product boxes like a cell phone or TV packaging, but the only thing you are doing is taking up space in your house. Instead, place the details and leaflets that you need inside a folder. This will save you space, and you will be able to find them more easily if you ever need them.

Your Quick Start Action Step:

When trying to figure out where to start when decluttering, begin with the room that bothers you the most. You may get an overwhelming feeling when you start because you have just too much clutter. These tips will help you get started:

- When you begin organizing one area, begin by throwing away the trash.

  Every room in a house is going to have trash in it. Look for broken pieces, expired coupons, empty containers, and dried-up glue. Getting rid of the trash first will help you concentrate on the rest of the clutter.

- For some unknown reason, all

things wind up in the kitchen.

Before you begin arranging your cabinets, get things that don't belong in the kitchen out of it. Make a pile of things that go into other rooms. Make sure you make a pile for each room. Take the appropriate things to the right rooms, and leave them there.

Something that most people don't think about checking is their spice rack. Head to your kitchen and go through your spices to check their expiration dates. You may be shocked to see that you have quite a few out-of-date spices.

Once you've gone through your

spices, head to your cupboard and have a look at the best-by dates on your bottles of sauces. Anything that you find that is out-of-date, get rid of it. Anything that you find that is getting close to the best-by date, position them at the front of your cabinet so that you know that they need to be used first.

Training yourself to do these on a regular basis will help you to save some time in the future.

You're not done in the kitchen just yet. Check to see if you have any plastic silverware. Look to see if you have any of those plastic bags of fork, knife, and napkin. Unless you entertain a lot of people or you eat on the go, you aren't going to need these things cluttering up your drawers. You probably already have proper silverware as well. Recycle these items.

While you're at it, get rid of condiment packets. Nobody ever uses the extra packets of ketchup. Buy a full-size bottle of the stuff and use it. It takes up a lot less space.

While you are cleaning out your fridge, get rid of leftovers that have been in there for more than five days. Throw out any food storage containers that have missing pieces. That missing lid isn't going to turn up, so just throw away the bowl.

- All magazines and reading
  materials end up in the living
  room.

  It gets moved around all over the
  place when you look for the
  remote. It might end up outdated,
  dusty, spilled on, and bent. It
  becomes something nobody
  wants to see. This can be
  eliminated when you can
  straighten up the piles of papers.
  A nice and neat pile looks like it is
  supposed to be there.

- Work on your bathroom one shelf
  or drawer at a time.

  Throw out all items that have

been used up or expired. Some medicines are still effective, but you are trying to declutter. The important thing to remember is that there are right and wrong ways to get rid of these things. You don't want to just toss them down the drain or into your garbage can. You can even contact a pharmacy for suggestions if you need to, but there are a lot of resources online.

- The home office is bad at holding onto bunches of clutter.

Get rid of items that you aren't working on anymore. Begin with stuff you have tried to keep until you find the part you need. If it hasn't been found by now, it never will. If you have no idea where a cord goes to, toss it. If you have newspapers that are more than two days old, get rid of them. Also, do you really need that rubber band ball?

Get a scrap piece of paper, and test all of your pens. Throw out those that don't work. Most people don't bother buying refills for pens, so there's no sense in keeping a pen that you've already replaced.

Get rid of last year's calendar. People hang onto calendars for a myriad of reason. The two biggest are that they think the pictures in it are cute, or that they are going to transfer important dates to their new calendar. Keep the calendar until January 31st, and if you haven't done anything with it by that time, toss it.

There is a constant theme throughout. Begin with obvious trash, lower the volume of materials, and focus on what is left in the area one section at a time.

Chapter 9: The "Less is More" Lifestyle for Debt-Free and Stress-Free Living

9.1

Being debt-free is a great feeling.
Getting to this point is very hard. What's
even harder is staying free of debt.

It can be done with dedication and hard
work. Getting control of your money and
controlling how and where you spend it
is priceless.

In today's society, being in debt is
normal. When someone says they have
gotten and stayed out of debt, it is just
too crazy for most people to believe. You
are definitely swimming upstream. But
the big question is: is it worth it?

- Sacrifice is empowering: You may
  have to work more than one job,
  and trudge through a job that you

don't really like—but knowing you are going to come out a winner will make it worth it. Becoming debt-free means you will have financial freedom, inner peace, and obviously more money. There are other benefits as well. The largest advantage of sacrificing and getting to your goal is knowing you have followed through and are able to reap the rewards. When you have to face a hard life choice or financial problem, you will know that you have the ability to handle whatever is thrown at you.

- Being financially free may get boring. Before you get rid of your debt, making decisions can consist of complicated strategies and many questions like: do I take a vacation, pay off the credit card, what do I pay first, and what card has the highest interest rate? Decisions are a lot easier. Pay the bills, put extra money into investing or savings, and use any money left over for other goals or entertainment. When you are debt-free, making decisions is a bit boring. You won't have any complicated spreadsheets. You are just living within your budget. If you absolutely love living on the edge, you will see when you have complete control over your finances that your life isn't as much exciting anymore. Slow and steady really does win the race. In this world of crazy financial ventures and endless promotions, the road to freedom is really boring.

- Getting back into debt is easy. You may soon see that your life after the debt is boring. Everything you encounter tempts you to spend more, and you find it hard to say no. This is very true when you have paid off all your credit cards, and they are upping your credit limit constantly. It is crazy to think it is super easy to put a few charges on your credit card, and then all of a sudden you are thousands of dollars in debt. There are some credit cards with good deals if you absolutely can't live without one. Some credit cards give you thousands of airline miles for charging a specific amount each month. If you can pay these off quickly, this is a great way to get free plane tickets. Even if you are disciplined enough to get out of debt, you must be disciplined enough to stay out. Just because you have everything paid off, doesn't mean you won't get the urge to buy things.

- It will feel like an uphill battle. Many people don't talk about life without debt, but it is like a slap in the face when reality kicks in. Just going to the store and buying groceries may scare you to death. You may constantly wonder if you have spent too much. The constant fear of going back into debt will creep into your mind. You have worked very hard to get free from debt, but you may realize that living a life without debt in it is very hard. It is an uphill battle constantly. You will still have moments where you wonder if you are going to be able to pay your bills or if you can actually afford that trip you promised the kids. Then the old worry about making enough money creeps into your mind. It doesn't matter if you are living your life after a debt or just trying to pay off your debts—you have to spend money in order to survive. This means that it will be a day-to-day struggle. The economy doesn't worry about the people who are trying to find their financial path without being in debt. The economy isn't nice to people who are trying to swim upstream. Then life hits you with these questions:

- o Will I really be able to save money?
- o Will it be enough?
- o Will I ever have true financial freedom from creditors and banks?

- Will it be worth it? Even though you have all these questions going through your head and struggle with them each day, you are still going to live a life free from debt. You don't let banks or creditors control your life—you control it. It doesn't matter how scary this may sound; it should fill your heart with hope.

- The truth about life after the debt is that once the excitement of being debt-free wears off, you will find there are downsides to being debt-free. Most people don't talk about it. So what is this downside? It is the fear of going back into debt. Everywhere you turn, you are going to encounter loan or credit card applications being thrown at you. People are going to try to persuade you to spend money you don't want to. It will get overwhelming. Society, in general, is geared to being in debt and staying there for their entire lives. It is a daily struggle to remain debt-free since this idea isn't normal in mainstream life. People are going to look at you like you have two heads when you constantly say no. Knowing you are going to have financial freedom and will be able to overcome all financial obstacles will give you all sorts of possibilities to have a life that is worth living free from debt. This sort of freedom will be totally worth it.

9.2

You may be wondering what the benefits of paying off your debts are. The most common are: freedom to spend the money any way you want, not having to live paycheck-to-paycheck, and having more money available in your accounts.

Are there other benefits to being free from debt? Yes, there are. Here are some great benefits to being debt-free:

- No more mental and physical stress: When you are dealing with huge amounts of debt, you may realize that you have many health problems. Four major health problems come from stress. These are lower respiratory problems, cancer, stroke, and heart disease. The biggest factor is your financial stress. When you can pay your debt down, you are going to reduce your mental and physical stressors. This will help you become a happier and healthier person.

- Relationships will be better: Most

people who fight or end up divorced say the reason behind it was almost always money. When you can reduce your debt, you are getting rid of the largest factor that causes stress in a relationship. Studies have shown that couples who are happy in their marriage do live longer than unhappy married people, divorced people, and single people. Less or no debt will mean you have less to fight about. This will lead to a more harmonious relationship. Your relationship will be more successful, plus you will find the relationship with your parents and children will also improve.

- Funding your dreams will be

attainable: Getting rid of debt gives you an opportunity to give, save, and spend the way you want to. You will finally be able to have that dream vacation you've always wanted. You may need new furniture—guess what? You can now go out and buy what you want. Achieving financial freedom allows you and your money to have your goals and dreams, instead of making somebody else's account bigger. You are no longer in debt to creditors for the rest of your life. You will be able to have fun and take risks.

- You will finally have peace of mind. Having this is absolutely priceless. There is nothing in the world better than having peace of mind. When you lay down at night and you know that you can take care of your family, that you can send your child to the college of their dreams, and that your job is the one you truly love—these benefits are easily attainable when you aren't in debt. You may not see them on paper, but life is more than just a math problem. When you start paying off your debts, you may experience these great side effects.

9.3

Most of this debt you have accumulated was for nothing. It just financed a short-lived lifestyle that vanished in a couple of years. Why does this happen? Most people believe that in order to live a modern life, you have to be in debt to do it.

Here are a few things that you can start doing now to help you gain control of your finances:

- Don't buy things you will forget quickly. If what you want to do or buy is something that you will just forget in a week, it isn't worth spending the money on. The only things you need to spend money on are your essential basic needs like shelter, clothing, and food. You may like doing memorable events such as having coffee each morning with friends—but you do this every day until it just isn't that enjoyable anymore. It has become normal and totally forgettable. Now, you are faced with an added expense where you are completely throwing money down the drain. Special purchases may even become totally forgettable. That book you have looked forward to reading is special but what about the 20th one? It is just put on the shelf with the rest.

- Look at your financial statement and find these unnecessary purchases. Did you make any purchases that you don't even remember making? Look for where you have spent the most money, and realize these are very wasteful purchases. Stay away from such places.

- Stay away from foods that are convenient. There is absolutely nothing wrong with taking your significant other out to a nice restaurant if it is for a memorable occasion like an anniversary or getting together with friends you haven't seen in a long time. It becomes a problem when you are just running short of time and swing into a drive-thru just to save you some time. These meals become totally forgettable. These meals are completely unhealthy, expensive, and really don't even save you much time. This also holds true for gas stations and convenience stores. You may be extremely thirsty or hungry when taking a road trip. This is why packing some snacks and drinks is so important.

- Take public transportation when you can. This isn't saying you must not own a car. Everybody has different living situations, and some may *need* a car. If you live in a rural area, you pretty much need a car to get places. If it is possible, your mode of transportation can be something that isn't as expensive as a car. A car must be a backup. What are these other modes of transportation? They are your feet, your bicycle, and public transportation. Cars can get expensive, even when they are paid for in full. There is parking, gas, maintenance, registration, and insurance. These can add up fast. If you can live without a car, you will be better off. If you absolutely need to have a car, think about buying a used one. Drive it until it is falling apart, then swap it for another used one.

- Go to the local library for entertainment. Most people think a local library is a place with angry librarians that tell everybody to hush. It is just row after row of dusty shelves full of old books. Obviously, they haven't been inside a library in an extremely long time. Libraries today have books for every reader, including children and adults. You will find educational books and page turners in every genre you can imagine. They even have DVDs of every genre as well. Some will have audiobooks available as well as equipment you can borrow. The great news here is it is all free. You only have to pay if you turn them in late. When you get tempted to rent or buy an audiobook, DVD, or book, check out your local library instead especially if you aren't sure you if are going to like it. Rent it for free before spending the money to buy it.

- Outdoor hobbies can serve many purposes. It gets you out and moving. This is great for your health. You are going to feel better, keep your medical problems away, and have more energy. Many outdoor hobbies aren't expensive. You are just going to need shoes and some time—and perhaps some equipment like soccer or other types of balls. Another reason for outdoor hobbies is that they are very social. You can become a part of a ball team and make new friends. You may even start collecting things like rocks, shells, or photographs. I have a close friend who collects heart-shaped rocks when she goes hiking with her grandchildren. I love taking pictures of nature that I put into calendars for presents.

Your Quick Start Action Step:

When you get out of debt, it is very tempting to start spending again. You are going to start getting all sorts of preapproved credit cards in the mail. Throw these in the trash. Track your spending. Just because you don't have any debt, doesn't mean you can spend your money without thinking about it. You don't necessarily have to stick to a strict budget. You do have to monitor your spending. By doing this, you will keep a feel for your spending. Once you get into the habit of looking through your financial statements, you will be able to feel that you are spending too much money.

A key for success in living free from debt is to change your expectations. Adopt a mentality where the money you are saving is worth more to you than that item you think you can't live without. You don't need the newest model of smartphone. You've only had the one you've gotten for a couple of months. Use it until it starts messing up, then trade in for a newer model. Each time you check your savings account, and it has gained interest, this must excite you more than buying that new computer or those new shoes that you really don't need.

Appreciate what you have. This is a very important step. Look around you, and take pride in what you possess. Look at your computer, television, furniture, car, and house. Now, look at nonphysical things like electricity, heat, air conditioning, and wireless network. As long as your health is good, you have the world. There is so much in life that you can look forward to. It doesn't matter how poor you feel right now—think about the less fortunate people in third world countries that would give anything to experience what you have right now. Being happy doesn't necessarily mean spending a lot of money. Just focus on what you have now and treasure them.

Bonus Chapter: Tips on Dealing with Large Expenses

10.1

In this day and age, financial tips are needed to stick to a budget and save money. When we are faced with a lot of information, we start asking the common question: "Where do I start?" For many, there are five areas that will take over 50 percent of our money. This is the best place to start.

These areas are retirement, education, children, car, and home. Let's see what we need to do:

- You need to feed a retirement fund. The amount of money you need to put aside to be able to retire is based on a simple equation of taking your current yearly income and multiply by 25.

If your take-home pay for the year is $60,000, and you want to be able to still live comfortably off that—you are going to need a retirement fund of $1,500,000. If you know this number early in your career, this will help you realize the importance of having this savings plan.

- Do you have to ask yourself how much is too much for a good education? People used to think it was fine to be in debt for student loans and a mortgage. Any other debt was considered bad debt. This isn't true now. We have figured out that too much of anything is actually bad. One rule of thumb is to not accrue more education debt than you will earn in the first ten years after you have graduated from both college and graduate school. Basically, if you know your job is going to give you around $60,000 a year, never exceed this amount in student loans. The logic here is that if it is going to take you over ten years to pay ten percent of your income each year in repaying loans, it will be hard to pay your other bills.

- Children can be expensive. The Department of Agriculture has estimated that it costs around $220,000 to raise a child from diapers to the age of 18. This is before the cost of education we listed above. Making the decision of becoming a parent is a large financial obligation.

- Your vehicles can drive you into a poor house. Many can usually afford to have a car that is about one-third of their total income for the year. If you make $50,000, you can easily have a car that costs $16,500. This may seem low, but this is why most people have financial problems. They drive it every day. Cars have a lot of other costs other than the monthly payment. You have to pay for maintenance, parking, gas, insurance, and many others. If you want to save money, the cost of transportation needs to be ten percent or lower of your annual income.

- How much of a house will you be able to comfortably afford? Many people use the rule of thumb where the purchase price of their home doesn't cost more than three times their yearly income. Maintaining a home is more than just your mortgage payment. You also have the upkeep, insurance, and property tax. These things can run you another two to three percent of the cost of your home every year. If you put 20 percent down on a 30-year fixed mortgage, your interest rate is around five to six percent, then three times your income will turn to about 30 percent of your total yearly income.

10.2

Cost of living is how much money you are going to need to live within a certain means. This includes healthcare, taxes, food, and housing. Most people use cost of living to figure out if they will be able to live in a certain city as opposed to another one. This is connected to your wages since salary is a measure of what is needed to keep up your normal mode of living in certain geographic regions.

Cost of living is a major factor when talking about accumulating personal wealth since a small salary can go further in cities where everything is relatively cheaper. If you have a larger salary, you may be able to live in a bigger, more expensive city. In a 2015 cost of living survey, the most expensive cities to live in were New York City,

Copenhagen, Zurich, Hong Kong, Geneva, Moscow, Osaka, and Tokyo. Cities within the United States that had the highest cost of living were San Francisco, Washington, Los Angeles, and Honolulu.

10.3

Creating a monthly budget usually makes sense. You have to set aside money to pay for student loans, utilities, mortgage or rent, and all the other bills you have, right? The big problem with some expenses like that vacation you want to take at the end of the school year, your friend's wedding in Aruba, and shopping for holidays only come up occasionally (like, once a year).

How can you put them into your

monthly budget? Use these guidelines to help you stay on track:

- Plan Ahead: At the start of every year, sit down and plan when you are going to take your vacation days. Most people only have a specific number available each year. Planning a budget is similar. If you already know you are going to your friend's wedding, allocate money for the cost of the dress, plane tickets, wedding gifts, and miscellaneous expenses once you get there. You have to figure out how much you need to save. Take this number and divide it by the number of paychecks you will get before then. This will tell you how much you need to take out of each check to cover this expense.

Let's not forget the expenses you have every year like car insurance. If you pay the entire premium when it comes due every six months, you can budget the amount out of each check to cover that cost as well.

- Figure Out Places to Save: After you have figured out the amount of money you need to get you through the year, you can look into some options. If you are good at keeping track of your budget, it is perfectly fine to put the money you need to save each month into a separate account and transfer it over when you need to pay a bill. It may be better to create different accounts for every expense like a holiday fund, computer fund, or vacation fund. This way, you can keep track of how much you have set aside for each and if you are reaching your target. Check with your financial institution, and see if they offer accounts such as a Christmas Club that will help you stay honest. You can put money into it all through the year; it penalizes you if you take money out before a specific date.

- Emergency Account: You need to put money into an emergency account for just that— emergencies. This will keep you from having to drain another account if you are faced with an unexpected expense. Some experts recommend having the amount of around three to six months of your total living expenses if you have an emergency such as repairs to your house or car, hospital stays, or losing a job. It may be tempting to tap into this account but *don't*. This money is *only* for emergencies. If you start skimming a little bit of money from this account here and there, you may find yourself in big trouble if an emergency were to actually arise.

- Don't Use Credit Cards: This is like dipping into the emergency account. A credit card can become a threat to your finances. It is okay to place a big purchase on a card to get you those airline miles, rewards, or even cash back—but you need to be sure you have put this into your monthly budget. You need to make sure you can pay it off in just a couple of months. If you begin paying interest each month, that wonderful deal will cost you a lot more than you have budgeted for.

When you plan ahead for all your expenses—including the less common and larger ones—you will be able to feel secure in knowing that you have the money to cover everything.

Your Quick Start Action Step

Put your plans on a calendar. You don't head out on vacation without knowing exactly where you are going. You need to do the same for your money. Get a calendar and sit down with your spouse or significant other, and put any irregular expenses you think you may encounter this year on it. These may include holidays, school supplies, tag renewals, vacation, and insurance. Write down how much you will need for each, and put this figure on the calendar when it will be due.

Once you know what to expect, you now need to put these into your budget monthly. For every expense, divide how much you need by how many months you have until the payment is due. Add this result to your monthly budget. You may have realized that when your load is light, it is easier to move around. The same goes for your finances. If your expenses are small, your money will go further. It seems worthwhile to find ways to cut down your expenses.

Insurance premiums are always a large amount of money that comes up usually every six months. Many insurance companies offer ways to save your money if you bundle your home and auto insurance together at the same premium. This can save you hundreds of dollars every six months.

The hardest part of planning a budget is figuring out how much money you need to set aside for unexpected expenses. Once you practice this awhile, it will become natural. Just use the tips above, and you will soon find you have more money than you realize.

Conclusion

Now that you've read *Minimalist Budget: How to Achieve Financial Success & Solve Debt with Simple Money Strategies to Positively Transform and Simplify Your Life*, you are well prepared to overhaul your spending habits with a proactive and optimistic mindset for your future. The key to creating a minimalist budget is to rewire your thinking from the lack of cash flow and resources. This way of thinking haunts most Americans whenever a bill or financial emergency strikes to a grounded and value-based mindset that will steer you confidently in the direction of your dreams. Your budget must reflect your true values, both in the short-term and long-term. Making daily spending choices that are influenced by your authentic self will free you from that icky, guilt-ridden feeling of buyer's remorse—or worse, the dull pang of knowing you must have been paying better attention to your finances. Life is never about money, and this book explores the very human dilemma of how to both provide for your lifestyle while investing in your future. The great reward is finding your true power, not in possessions and extraneous expenses, but in yourself. No matter how dire your financial situation is, no matter how impossible it may seem to get yourself out of your financial hole, no matter how many times friends and family members may have written you off as a lost cause—you are not alone, and you can fully financially recover. The step-by-step instructions at the end of each chapter will guide you and immediately impact your financial health for the better. Set yourself free from debt and worry by embracing the power you have to choose to live simply, smartly, and with the *Minimalist Budget* mindset.

Finally, if this book has given you value and has helped you in any way, then I'd like to ask you for a favor if you would be kind enough to leave a review for this book on Amazon? It'd be greatly appreciated!

Thank you and good luck!

Preview Of 'Declutter Your Mind' by Marie S. Davenport

Chapter 3: Why your Mind is Filled with Clutter - And How to Fix It

3.1 **Your brain on clutter**

Described as anything that is kept, even though not used, needed or wanted, clutter can also be defined as having a disorganized and overwhelming amount of possessions in our living space, cars or storage areas. But clutter isn't just physical. When you have to-do items constantly floating around in your head, or you hear a ring every few minutes from your phone, your brain doesn't get a chance to fully enter creative flow or process experiences. Clutter creates stress that has three major biological and neurological effects on us—our cortisol levels, our creativity and ability to focus, and our experience of pain.

The overconsumption of digital stuff— like social media notifications, news feeds, games and files on our computer—competes for our attention, creating a digital form of clutter that has the same effect on our brain as physical clutter. Neatness and order support health—and oppose chaos.

So, what is going on? Our brains love order. The human body consists of thousands of integrated and interdependent biological and neurochemical systems, all organized and operating along circadian rhythms, without which our bodies would disintegrate into chaos. It's no wonder that the organization within our very own bodies naturally extends to the desire for order and tidiness in our homes. And order feels good, in part, because it's easier for our brains to deal with and not have to work so hard.

3.2 The science of cortisol

No matter the ways, reasons, and means by which the creep of stuff exceeds our ability to mentally and physically manage it—all of it amounts to stress. Clutter can trigger the release of the stress hormone cortisol, which can increase tension and anxiety and lead to unhealthy habits. Cortisol is a hormone produced in response to stress by the hypothalamus-pituitary-adrenal axis (HPA).

Chronic clutter can create prolonged stress, throwing us into a state of low-grade, perpetual fight-or-flight—the system designed to help us survive. The fight-or-flight response involves the complex interaction of many body systems and organs that activate needed functions and minimize unnecessary functions during times of stress. These systems must remain in balance to maintain optimum physical and psychological health.

According to a Cornell University study from 2016, stress triggered by clutter may also trigger coping and avoidance strategies, like eating junk food, oversleeping or binge-watching Netflix.

If we are not stressed, we get most of our cortisol in the morning to get us going. Levels taper off the rest of the day if we are relaxed, enabling us to enjoy psychological and physical wellbeing. But a messy home environment can prevent our body's cortisol levels from naturally declining throughout the day. Taxing this system eventually results in higher levels of depression and anxiety, and a lower capacity to think clearly, make decisions, and stay focused.

To supply the body with the energy needed to deal with stress, there are several physiological changes that occur with elevated cortisol levels:

- Diversion of blood flow to the muscles from other parts of the body
- Increased blood pressure
- Increased heart rate
- Increased blood sugars
- Increased fats in in the blood

If there is no relief from stress, all of these changes are bad for healthy brain activity and can cause lasting negative changes in brain function and structure. Additionally, when stress raises the body's cortisol levels, its overall health can be adversely affected, including organ damage, the suppression of the immune, endocrine and reproductive systems, the lowering of the metabolism, and the disruption of the sleep cycle, to name a few.

It is difficult to maintain a state of wellness over time when the body's energy is channeled into coping with stress.

Just as concerning, when the body is in a state of chronic stress and not thinking clearly, the brain tends to only see that which is negative as these are, historically, the things that could turn into threats. Unfortunately, all this does is reinforce the pre-existing sour point of view, perceived lack of social support and subsequent poor interrelationships.

Research from a 2009 study out of UCLA's Center on Everyday Lives of Families (CELF) has shown that women who perceive their homes to be cluttered tend to have unhealthy patterns of cortisol levels. A team of professional archaeologists, anthropologists, and other social scientists studied the home life of 32 middle-class, dual-income families with 2-3 children of ages 7-12 in Los Angeles. In the study, family members recorded self-directed home tours describing objects and spaces in their homes, during which saliva samples were taken at regular intervals to measure cortisol levels.

The data were collected for three days and compared to and correlated with vast amounts of other data previously collected over the course of four years. According to the CEFL study, the amount of stress women experience at home is directly proportional to the amount of stuff they and their family had accumulated.

It's interesting to note in the UCLA study that men did not exhibit the same results, having normal cortisol fluctuations. Presumably, they were not as stressed by the amount of stuff in their home. This can be explained possibly by the results of other studies that have shown that the home is traditionally perceived as women's domain and ultimate responsibility, even in households where both partners work.

Other studies also support the finding that if men don't think the responsibility of keeping the house tidy is relevant to them, they may not be inclined to see the clutter and so are not as stressed about it.

This may be explained further in part by research that has indicated that there are distinct differences in vision between men and women since men have 25 percent more neurons in their visual cortex, a part of the cerebral cortex that processes visual information. The irony is that even though the visual cortex of a man has more neurons than a woman's, men are impacted more by the things they see that they think have to do with them, and less by the things they think do   not.

The brain has a limited capacity to process information. To filter out extra stimuli and focus on what we are trying to achieve at any given moment, the top-down and bottom-up attention mechanisms compete. By mutually suppressing each other, brain power is exhausted, and ultimately, we lose focus. Whether we know it or not, a kitchen counter stacked with mail and basket full of unfolded laundry can be as distracting to us as a toddler in the throes of a tantrum.

3.3 **Start to declutter**

Now that we know what all of our extra stuff is doing to our health and ability to function, it's time to get rid of it, right?... Oh, but if it were only that easy. Although most people don't experience heightened ACC/Insula activity to this degree, we can all identify with the feeling of angst when finally tossing that pile of unread magazines, or those ticket stubs from last summer's trip to New York to see Hamilton. The good news is, those who suffer from hoarding respond well to Cognitive Behavioral Therapy. For the rest of us... there is decluttering.

In addition to improving your mood and focus, decluttering often acts as a catalyst for taking better care of other aspects of our life. By purging unneeded items from our homes, it is like deleting files to create disk space on your computer. Suddenly, the whole operating system is more efficient...this decreases stress and increases your effectiveness personally and professionally.

While actually going ahead and getting rid of unnecessary items will be covered in detail in a later chapter, the exercises in this chapter are going to cover the preparation you will need to do in order to get ready to declutter once and for all. This lifestyle change requires two things: a vision list, and a why list. You will want to start with your vision list. This list is going to be everything you want to accomplish from your future results. Your list can, and should, contain anything that is important to you and serves as a reason for why you are making this lifestyle change. The more unique and personal this list is, the better it will serve you.

If you are having a hard time getting started, here are some things you might consider writing on your vision list:

- I want to eat healthier at every single meal

- I want to experience the loving relationships in my life, every day
- I want to contribute to the world in a meaningful way, daily
- I want to read and write on a daily basis
- I want to be passionate about every single day that I'm alive
- I want to take risks in life
- I want to be present in every single moment

These visions are essentially what you want to accomplish through your minimalist lifestyle. After you are clear on what you want to achieve with your new lifestyle, you want to get clear on why. Understanding why you want change is what will compel you to actually make the change. So, after you completely your list that outlines everything you want, you can start a list right beneath it that is going to tell you every reason why you want it. You should make sure that both lists are as detailed as possible. If you have several important items on your vision list, and on your why list, that is completely okay. You should not feel as though you have to limit yourself. The more reasons you can provide, the easier the entire transition is going to be for you.

As you become more aware of what you want, as well as why you want it you should find that it becomes easier and easier to motivate yourself to actually start working towards achieving your dreams. While you may feel as though your good intentions are strong enough to get you through right now, not listening to your mental clutter can be more difficult at the moment than you might expect. That is why it is important to have your vision and your why. These are lists you will refer back to when you are feeling internal resistances. You can regroup, refocus, and start all over again in a new frame of mind that will allow you to have an easier ability to achieve your desired results.

Your Quick Start Action Step: Start working on your vision list

As discussed above, your vision list is the linchpin that holds your motivation together. You don't need to put it together all at once, however, if you need some time to work on it that is perfectly fine. You can keep a running tally of things to add to it whenever you think of a new one. This process doesn't have to stop either, you can add something new to your vision list whenever the need strikes you.

Chapter 4: Effective Meditation - Being in the Present Moment

4.1 An ancient practice

Mindfulness meditation is a type of meditation which focuses on being as aware of each moment as possible, thereby helping the consciousness to expand by forming a stronger connection with the present. Mindfulness meditation has a long history of practice as part of the Buddhist faith where it is revered for its ability to improve both mental happiness and physical well-being. This has been corroborated by research which shows that mindfulness meditation is a beneficial treatment for a variety of mental conditions. What's more, it has also been shown to be effective when treating conditions including anxiety, stress and drug addiction.

While mindfulness can be practiced almost anywhere at nearly any time, the concept began as a structured meditation technique practiced by Buddhists known as vipassana. Roughly translated this means to live in the moment while understanding that sometimes you must be aware of the future as well. The general idea is that achieving vipassana will allow you to come to understand the universe as a whole and comes through the knowing of a few key principals.

The idea of practicing mindfulness first caught on in the Western world in the early part of the 1970s. Professor Jon Kabat-Zinn is credited with creating a mindfulness based method of stress reduction which paired mindfulness with yoga to great result. While Zinn didn't do anything particularly new, the fact that his techniques led to measurable improvements for a wide variety of ailments both mental and physical in turn led to additional studies on the topic. These studies have shown time and again how effective practicing mindfulness can be which in turn has led to a steady increase in the practice to the point where it can now be found being regularly practiced in schools, veteran treatment facilities, hospitals, even prisons.

4.2 **Many benefits**
In addition to helping improve self-discipline, studies show that that taking 15 minutes out of your day to practice mindfulness meditation has a host of additional benefits as well. For starters, it is known to show dramatic increases when it comes to projecting a strong sense of self while at the same time noticeably reducing stress. This is thanks to the positive effects that mindfulness meditation has on attention

span, emotional regulation and body awareness. What's even more impressive, neuroimaging has shown that mindfulness meditation actually allows those who practice it to process information more quickly than those who do not.

The activity can also literally improve the health of the brain as studies show that those who started practicing mindfulness meditation at a young age actually have more volume in their brains as they age. Meditating regularly is also known to increase the thickness of the hippocampus which means that it actually makes it easier to learn new information and retain it for a prolonged period of time. It also positively affects the amygdala which means those who meditate are less likely to experience stress, anxiety, and fear. With so much going on under the hood, is it any wonder that those who meditate tend to report an overall increase in mood, temperament, and wellbeing?

Beyond these noticeable physical changes, regularly practicing mindfulness is known to help improve self-discipline in additional ways by decreasing instances of meditators' minds getting stuck in negative thought patterns while also making it easier to focus for prolonged periods of time. A recent Johns Hopkins University study found that practicing mindfulness meditation regularly is equally effective at treating anxiety, depression, and ADHD as many commonly prescribed drugs.

Other reasons to practice mindfulness meditation

- Mindfulness meditation naturally leads to a deeper understanding of the self and allows many people to take stock of their strengths and weaknesses, leading to personal growth.

- Studies show that those who practice mindfulness regularly have a stronger memory, leading to an easier retention of facts in both the long and the short term.

- In addition to the specifics, mindfulness meditation improves overall physical wellbeing with those who practice regularly reporting fewer instances of illness and a more rapid recovery when they do fall ill.

- Mindfulness meditation can help improve emotional control while at the same time increasing one's threshold for pain.

- As surprising as it might seem, making a habit of being mindful can actually make even the most middling music seem more engaging. This deeper level of engagement leads to a general increase of enjoyment, regardless of the type of music or any previous musical preferences.

- With a regular dose of mindfulness meditation, many people experience a dramatic increase in their ability to empathize with others no matter what the situation. Furthermore, it allows practitioners to listen to other viewpoints more actively, more compassionately and results in their ability to withhold judgement on thoughts and ideas that differ from their own.

4.3

While practicing mindfulness meditation might seem like a tall order at first, the truth of the matter is that being mindful is a habit which means you can learn to improve through practice, practice, practice. In fact, it should be one of the easier habits in this book to get accustomed to as it is as easy as taking a few moments out of your day to focus exclusively on the present via all of the information that your senses are bringing in.

1. *Getting started:* When you first start practicing mindfulness, it is important to always practice at the same day to ensure your body is going to get into the habit of entering a mindful state each and every day, to make the transition easier to manage. Don't forget, it takes about a month for a new habit to solidify in your mind which means that as long as you can keep it up for that amount of time you can keep it up indefinitely.

In order to reach a state of mindfulness, you are going to want to find someplace comfortable, and quiet to sit, though not so quiet and comfortable that you are tempted to fall asleep. Then, all you need to do is breathe deeply, in and out. As you breathe in, focus all of your attention on the information that your senses are providing to you, focus on the way the air feels in your lungs, how it smells and how it tastes. Slowly but surely, expand your consciousness so that you are taking in as much information about your surroundings as possible.

2. *Observe the moment:* Mindfulness is not necessarily quieting the mind or finding an eternal state of calmness. The goal here is simple. We want to pay attention to the moment we are in without judging. When we

judge a thought or something we may have done in the past, we tend to dwell on it. That isn't living in the moment and is not conducive to mindful meditation. While this is easier said than done, it is a crucial step to mindful meditation. With practice, it will be easy to achieve. Be mindful of the moment, of your senses and your surroundings.

3. *Ignore those pesky judgments:* Take notice of the times you are passing judgment while practicing. Make note of them and move on.

4. *Always come back to observation and the present moment:* It is

easy for our minds to get lost in thought. Mindfulness meditation is the art of bringing yourself back to the moment, over and over, as many times as it takes. Don't get discouraged. In the beginning, you will find your mind wanders a lot. Reel it back in and keep moving forward.

5. *Be kind to yourself:* Even if your mind does happen to wander, and it will, don't be hard on yourself. It happens. Acknowledge whatever thoughts pop up, put them to the side and get back on track.

To learn more about "Declutter Your Mind" by Marie S. Davenport, visit the

Amazon website.

www.ingramcontent.com/pod-product-compliance
Lightning Source LLC
Chambersburg PA
CBHW061023220326
41597CB00019BB/3146